AUBREY COHEN COLLEGE LIBRARY
75 Varick St. 12th Floor
New York, NY 10013

People and Programs That Make a Difference in a Multicultural Society

Front Cover photos taken by Emma Thomas Pitts

PEOPLE AND PROGRAMS THAT MAKE A DIFFERENCE IN A MULTICULTURAL SOCIETY
Volunteerism in America

Emma Thomas Pitts

The Edwin Mellen Press
Lewiston•Queenston•Lampeter

Library of Congress Cataloging-in-Publication Data

Pitts, Emma Thomas.
    People and programs that make a difference in a multicultural society : volunteerism in America / Emma Thomas Pitts.
        p. cm.
    Includes bibliographical references.
    ISBN 0-7734-7946-5
    1. Voluntarism--United States Case studies. 2. Volunteers--United States Case studies. 3. Social action--United States Case studies. 4. Socially handicapped--Services for--United States Case studies. I. Title.
HN90.V64P57   1999
361.3' 7' 0973--dc21   99-27737
                                                                     CIP

A CIP catalog record for this book is available from the British Library.

Copyright © 1999 Emma Thomas Pitts

All rights reserved. For information contact

    The Edwin Mellen Press   The Edwin Mellen Press
          Box 450   Box 67
      Lewiston, New York   Queenston, Ontario
       USA 14092-0450   CANADA L0S 1L0

The Edwin Mellen Press, Ltd.
Lampeter, Ceredigion, Wales
UNITED KINGDOM SA48 8LT

Printed in the United States of America

TABLE OF CONTENTS

Chapter		Page
	Acknowledgements...	vi
	Foreword...	vii
	Charles Thomas, J.D.	
	Washington, D. C.	
	Poem..	x
	LaToya Wilson	
	Introduction..	1
1	Alabama..	5
	The Person(s): Bo Jackson	
	The Program(s): America Goes Back To School	
2	Arkansas..	9
	The Person(s): Sam Walton	
	The Program(s): Wal-Mart's Scholarships	
3	California..	13
	The Person(s): Mary Catherine Swanson	
	The Program(s): Streetcats Foundation	
	California Migrant Education Literature Project	
	DIAL III Standardization	
4	Connecticut...	19
	The Person(s): Paula Brown Edme	
	The Program(s): Waterbury Community Release Program	
5	Delaware...	23
	The Person(s): Marianne Locke	
	The Program(s): Jersey Cape Dance Center	

TABLE OF CONTENTS

Chapter   **Page**

6   Florida.. 27
        The Person(s): Ethel Koger Beckham
        The Program(s): North Dade Center for Modern Languages
                        Communities In School

7   Georgia... 33
        The Person(s): Rosa Arnold; Jermaine Dupri
        The Program(s): Tickets for Kids; Camp Sunshine

8   Hawaii.. 37
        The Person(s): Lafete Tucker, Sr.; Jane Campbell
        The Program(s): Speaking, Relating, and Learning
                        Indigenous Language Immersion Programs

9   Idaho... 43
        The Person(s): Marilyn Howard; Vincent Muli Wa Kituku
        The Program(s): Individualized Education Programs
                        Helping Homeless Families

10   Illinois... 49
        The Person(s): James T. Meeks; Kirby Puckett
        The Program(s): High Jump Program

11   Indiana... 55
        The Person(s): Chris Karimu
        The Program(s): Project SEED

12   Iowa... 59
        The Person(s): Shannon C'deBraca
        The Program(s): Iowa Child Abuse Prevention Program

13   Kansas... 63
        The Person(s): Emanuel Cleaver; Chris Whittle
        The Program(s): The Edison Project
                 Make-A-Wish Foundation
                 Midwestern Prevention Project

14   Kentucky.. 71
        The Person(s): Deborah Grubb; Jerry Abramson
        The Program(s): Child Watch
                 Student Technology Leadership Program

TABLE OF CONTENTS   iii

Chapter   Page

15   Louisiana... 77
     The Person(s): Margaret A. Brown; Darryl Kilbert
     The Program(s): Building Blocks; TAPSIS

16   Massachusetts... 83
     The Person(s): Marie McCormick; Mitchell Resnick
     The Program(s): Cops and Kids
              Hugh O'Brian Youth Leadership Foundation

17   Michigan... 89
     The Person(s): Mark Bos; Ronald E. Hall; Fannie Dell Peeples
     The Programs(s): The Economic Club of Detroit Scholarships
              Royal Readathon

18   Mississippi.. 95
     The Person(s): Oseola McCarty
     The Program(s): Mississippi School for Mathematics and Science

19   Missouri... 99
     The Person(s): Laurie Sybert
     The Program(s): A Hard Line for Learning

20   Montana... 103
     The Person(s): Chuck Hunter
     The Program(s): Curriculum Innovation: Middle School Approach

21   Nebraska.. 107
     The Person(s): Wolf Wolfensberger; Kim N. Lombardi
     The Program(s): Youth Services International, Inc.
              People's City Mission

22   New Hampshire.. 113
     The Person(s): Jeanne Shaheen
     The Program(s): Hampshire County Youth Service

23   New Jersey... 117
     The Person(s): Lauryn Hill; David Wiesner
     The Program(s): The Refugee Project

TABLE OF CONTENTS

Chapter		Page
24	New Mexico... The Person(s): Martin J. Chavez The Program(s): Little Kids, Big Projects	123
25	New York.. The Person(s): Antonio Pantoja The Program(s): The ASPIRA Association, Inc.	127
26	Pennsylvania.. The Person(s): Curtis Martin The Programs(s): Creating a Caring Community in Classrooms	131
27	Rhode Island.. The Person(s): Leona A. Kelly The Program(s): Rhode Island's Interactive Science Museum	135
28	South Carolina... The Person(s): Maggie Wallace Glover The Program(s): South Carolina Higher Education Tuition Grants	139
29	South Dakota... The Person(s): Judith E. Kroll; William J. Janklow The Program(s): Alcohol Free Kids; HUD Block Funds	143
30	Tennessee.. The Person(s): Elizabeth Swartz The Program(s): Network of Mindful Schools	149
31	Texas.. The Person(s): Joe and Elvia Rodriguez The Program(s): Accelerated Learning Center	153
32	Vermont.. The Person(s): Susan Brody Hasazi The Program(s): I-Team	157

TABLE OF CONTENTS

Chapter   **Page**

33   Virginia.. 161
       The Person(s): Jina Moore; Kevin Ward
       The Program(s): Healthy Schools
             Telephone Pioneers

34   Wisconsin... 167
       The Person(s): Marvin Schwan
       The Program(s): TRIO

       Appendix.. 171
       Programs Designed to Help People

ACKNOWLEDGEMENTS

Many thanks to all of the men, women, and children who work untiringly 365 days a year to make this a better world. Their dedication, personal time, and personal financial contributions are unmatched.

I salute all of the wonderful people in this world who are making a difference.

Emma Thomas Pitts

FOREWORD

During my day-to-day encounters, I meet, work, and counsel with people from all walks of life throughout the United States and globally. There are good days and not so good days. Being that our physical differences are obviously apparent, there are many other kinds of "hidden" differences that must be acknowledged. The first step in identifying a problem is the know that there is a problem.

Abraham H. Maslow, a leading psychologist, identified some needs in his "Hierachy of Needs" that all human beings crave to satisfy; i.e. food, shelter, clothing, security, belongingness, and self actualization. Belongingness is defined by *Webster's Dictionary* as "to be classified." People have different ways of expressing these common needs, especially the need to belong. Some will do so constructively; others, destructively. I see much destruction in my line of work; low self-esteem, divorce, abuses of all kinds, violences, symptoms for violent behaviors, and many, many more. And for this very reason, I am in total agreement that "it does take a village" to succeed in this world.

Sometimes, when clients enter my office, I can see the rejection and pain written all over their faces. Even though they tend to make a concerted effort to conceal in some instances their unhappiness through a facade, and in other instances their acts of dissatisfaction toward themselves and others, it just doesn't work. There never is or will be enough research to handle all of the problems in this world (and believe me, there are quite a few!).

Dr. Pitts is making a difference through her research on multicultural education. As indicated in this book, bit by bit, people are beginning to realize that we all live in this world together and that what affects one, affects all. They are becoming more aware that small steps lead to big steps; that you don't have to be nationally known or financially well off to "steer" someone in the right direction.

All of us who are in the "people profession" know that we have to make many concessions daily to communicate effectively. One wrong word can trigger a negative reaction; one wrong move can prove to be deadly. The daily newspapers attest to the high statistics on crime that metropolitan, urban, and rural areas alike are experiencing. I alluded to the "people profession." But there is no escape in making contact with people everywhere we are.

The book begins each chapter with some information about individual states. I find that knowing something about a person's environment helps me to understand why a person acts or communicates the way he does. People who are unaware of mores, norms, and customs tend to retaliate toward every move, word, and gesture. A lack of understanding is one reason why the list of clientele in my practice is ever growing. The book's format continues with information about people and programs. This compilation provides a starting point and serves as an incentive for other persons to become well informed about their counterparts, as well as getting started themselves.

It is particularly refreshing to read about the commonality that churches, corporations, celebrities, academicians, entrepreneurs, students of all ages, lay people, parents, and others in their respective communities share in wanting to contribute to humanity. I am alluding to Dr. Pitts' introduction—the truck driver who sends postcards anonymously to nursing home residents, the eleven-year-old who operates her own café for children, the husband and wife who opened their home to eight siblings after a promise they made to the children's dying mother, the governmental worker who is known as "Dr. Fox" because of his generosity, just to cite a few. These kinds of human interest stories bring out the spark in all of us to get off of our laurels and start working!

FOREWORD

The Appendix is very thorough and valuable. It serves as an excellent source for additional references.

I believe, without a doubt, this research will carry us into the new millennium with hope and anticipation for a better world.

Charles Thomas, J.D.
Washington, D. C.

ACCEPTANCE

Acceptance is a feeling of belonging,
Acceptance is a feeling of closeness,
Acceptance is needed for togetherness.

Because skin tones and colors are different,
Because physical attributes are different,
Because emotional needs are different,
Everyone is different. Accept it!

Do not deny things one cannot handle,
Do not fight battles against differences that cannot be changed,
Accept those differences that shape the world.

Remember, when the skin is pricked,
The red fluid that flows is the same color.
When emotions run high,
The clear fluid that flows from the eyes is the same color.

Acceptance is a feeling of belonging,
Acceptance is a feeling of closeness,
Acceptance is needed for togetherness.

LaToya Wilson
©Copyright 1999 by LaToya Wilson
Permission Granted

INTRODUCTION

"Pass a little kindness and your life gets better," declares Oprah Winfrey, queen of the talk show circuit and host of her own television series, **The Oprah Winfrey Show**. Many people nationwide are extending helping hands to the less fortunate in an effort to "clean up" and make America better. Sometimes all that is needed is a listening ear, a kind word, a helping hand....Plagued with violence, teen pregnancies, drugs, physical and emotional disabilities, cultural differences, homelessness, and the list goes on, people are finding that not only are they sharing their many gifts and talents, but are making a difference at the same time.

Cassander Vann, 11, has her own Kids' Café in Springfield, Missouri in which she serves hot meals—soup and chili—to underprivileged children. There are no prerequisites. Children who are hungry just walk into the café and get served.

Otis and Barbara Green, 72 and 57, of Clearwater, Florida run a homeless shelter.

Jama Hedgecoth, 40, of Locust Grove, Georgia operates a safe haven and rehabilitation center for animals, as well as a group home for foster children.

Jon Wagner-Holtz, 17, of Mission Viejo, California founded Kids Konnected to offer friendship and support to the children of cancer victims.

Al and Rose Malavolti, 48 and 45, of Rockford, Illinois, parents of four, opened their home to eight siblings after their mother, bedridden and dying of stomach cancer, begged the couple to keep her children together.

A cross-state truck driver, who wants to remain anonymous, was featured on **Sunday Morning**, December 13, 1998 for his good deed of sending postcards to persons throughout the United States who are confined to nursing homes. He stated that he plans to remain anonymous because he does not want to be identified.

INTRODUCTION

In a special segment entitled "What Makes a School Great," on **Good Morning America**, the national television broadcast, the Renaissance School has a Club of Men consisting of male students who must have a 2.5 grade average to enter and a 3.0 to remain in the club. Teachers and parents lift students through high expectations. Teachers do not look at their involvement with the students as just a paycheck, but a lot of pride in the end result.

Red McComb, owner of the Minnesota Vikings, personally visits Mary Hall Elementary School and contributes time to talk with the students. The school has been nationally recognized for academic excellence.

Kareem Abdul Jabbar, retired National Basketball Association star, volunteers as a high school coach at the White Mountain Apache Reservation.

Andrea Jaeger, tennis star, in her program Kids Stuff Foundation, brings 20 kids diagnosed with terminal illnesses together at the Kids Stuff Silver Lining Ranch in Aspen, Colorado to meet celebrities, play games, eat pizza, and support for each other.

Al Fox, governmental worker, Washington, D. C., in his program, Community Youth Connection, Incorporated is on his volunteer job 365 days a year assisting five area schools with donations like a $150 shopping spree at local malls, supplying children with shoes, eyeglasses, etc. Sears Department stores recently donated $400 to his program. The children call him "Dr. Fox." He assists non-school children alike.

The Van Dykes of Iowa participated in a program spearheaded by Simon Estes designed to put African children in American host homes. Naomi and Cee Cee of Cape Cod, Africa spent one year with the Van Dykes. The hosts and participants learned from each other.

Inmates at Angola State Prison, Angola, Louisiana make more than 5,000 toys for needy children annually during the Christmas holidays.

Whether it is the well known such as First Lady of the United States Hillary Rodham Clinton or a lesser known such as Alexene Baker of Gonzales, Louisiana, who is an advocate for battered women, people seem to be in agreement that love has no

INTRODUCTION 3

boundaries. They are using their God-given talents and resources not to put their names in lights, but to bring light into the lives of others. These volunteers do not dwell on monetary compensation, but the positive effects their programs are making and the sheer exuberance when they see smiles on people's faces.

Anne Frank, **The Diary of Anne Frank**, states that "in spite of everything, I really believe that people are good people." Red McComb believes "the measure of a man is the size of his heart."

The people and programs featured in this book attest that **people and programs do make a difference in a multicultural society.**

Emma Thomas Pitts

CHAPTER 1

The State: Alabama

The state of Alabama boasts a population today consisting of a white population of 2,975,837, African American population of 1,020,677, urban population of 1,601,038, and a rural population of 1,061,378. About two-thirds of the people of Alabama live in metropolitan areas. About a fourth of the people are blacks. Other large populations in the state include people of Irish, English, German, and American Indian descent. It entered the union on December 14, 1819.

Cities such as Birmingham, Huntsville, Mobile, and Montgomery have kept the attractiveness of small communities in spite of their rapid growth. Hugh oak trees arch over wide boulevards, even in many downtown areas. Stately old homes add to the charm and dignity of these cities; thus, creating a picturesque look. Mobile, on Mobile Bay, is Alabama's only seaport.

The **Mobile Register**, founded in 1813, is Alabama's oldest newspaper.

Famous Alabamians include Booker T. Washington, The Commodores of Motown Recording Agency at Tuskegee University, Nat King Cole, Hank Williams, Charles Barkley, Latrell Spreewell, and Bo Jackson.

Alabama's capital is Montgomery. The state bird is the yellowhammer; the flag is a crimson cross of St. Andrew; the motto is "We Dare Defend Our Rights"; and the official mascot is the eastern tiger.

The Person(s)

Mr. Bo Jackson

Bessemer. Mr. Bo Jackson is an African American who was born on November 30, 1962 in this small town. At the age of thirteen, he showed his first real talent in baseball by playing in an adult league. He was accepted to Auburn University on a sports scholarship in 1980. While going to Auburn, he played on the football, baseball, track, and field teams. Mr. Jackson dropped out of college to play pro football and baseball, but came back in 1992 and received his degree in 1993. The first sport he played was baseball for the Mets, but later decided to play football for the Raiders. An injury forced him out of football. But he still plays baseball for the Angels in California.

In addition to being in the public's eye as a well-known athlete, Mr. Jackson gives a lot of his time to the community as a public speaker. He serves as co-chair of "America Goes Back to School." Mr. Jackson is constantly encouraging various groups to get involved with the educating of our children. He is a strong advocate of education and believes that everybody should get involved.

He, along with other co-chairs, encourages parents, grandparents, community leaders, employers and employees, the military, members of the arts and scientific communities, students, religious leaders, and other caring citizens to work together and with schools and colleges to make education better and support learning in and outside the schools.

To emphasize the importance of this effort, he often travels to industry, schools, and other agencies as a public speaker on behalf of this initiative to gain financial, as well as moral support. Mr. Jackson has been lauded for his involvement in this initiative over and over again. He never ceases from getting involved with children and serving as an advocate for them.

The Program(s)

America Goes Back To School

Nationwide. America Goes Back To School is an initiative of the United States Department of Education and the Partnership for Family Involvement in Education. This organization represents more than 700 families, arts and education, business, religious and community groups that support family involvement in children's learning. It seeks to mobilize grassroots support for improved learning for all students during back to school time from August through October.

U. S. Secretary of Education Richard W. Riley listed the challenges in his first Annual State of American Education address which include:

- Make schools safe and disciplined: A precondition for learning
- Encourage parent and family involvement
- Make America a reading, literate society
- Reach for new levels of excellence: Achieve high standards and real accountability
- Make computers available so all students will succeed in the 21st Century
- Prepare young people for careers: A strong transition from school to work
- Make college more accessible: Keep the promise of the American dream

Education sponsors of the back to school initiative include: American Association of School Administrators; American Federation of Teachers; Council for American Private Education; Council of Chief State School Officers; National Association of Elementary School Principals; National Association of Secondary School Principals; National Coalition for Parent Involvement in Education; National Coalition of Title I/Chapter I Parents; and National Education Association.

Co-chairs include Tipper Gore, athlete and businessman Bo Jackson, National PTA president Joan Dykstra, and Southern Illinois University president Ted Sanders.

♦ ♦ ♦
References

Alabama. *World book encyclopedia.* (1994 ed.).

Davis, J. Non-game birds in Alabama. Wildlife Section, Game, and Fish Division, Alabama State Department of Conservation and Natural Resources, n.d.

Website

http://www.asc.edu/archives/emblems/st_bird.html

CHAPTER 2

The State: Arkansas

The state of Arkansas is known as the **Natural State**. It was named for Native Americans of the **Arkansa** or **Quapaw** tribe, who were numerous in the region before the coming of white settlers.

According to the 1990 census, Arkansas has 2,350,725 inhabitants. Whites constitute 82.7 percent of the population and blacks, 15.9 percent; additional population groups include 12,733 Native Americans and 12,530 people of Asian or Pacific Island origin. Nearly 20,000 Arkansas residents are of Hispanic origin. The largest religious denominations are Baptist and Methodist.

Bill Clinton, who became president of the United States in 1993, was born in Arkansas and has lived there for much of his life.

Arkansas has 75 counties, each of which is administered by a county judge. By most standards, Arkansas is one of the poorest states in the United States. The state figure of $12,691 in 1993 was 22 percent below the U. S. average.

The state's major rivers are the Mississippi, St. Francis, White, Arkansas, Red, Ouachita, and their tributaries.

The state capital is Little Rock, which is also the largest city. The state bird is the mockingbird; the state tree, pine; the state flower, apple blossom; the state drink, milk; and the state motto "The People Rule!"

The Person(s)

Mr. Sam Walton

Bentonville. Mr. Sam Walton grew up during the depression and knew that hard work and thrift were a way of life. He was described as industrious, always trying to get the most out of money, and had a burning ambition to succeed.

Mr. Walton was born on March 29, 1918 to Thomas Gibson and Nancy Lee Walton. As he grew up, anyone could see how determined he was to succeed and as time passed he went from being a poor town boy to the richest man in the world.

In 1950 Mr. Walton purchased a store in Bentonville, Arkansas, which ended up being called Walton's 5 & 10. This store was also a member of the Butler Brothers' Ben Franklin chain. Before this store opened it needed many improvements, but to Mr. Walton that was no problem. He was never discouraged for a second. To introduce his store to the new town in July 1950, Mr. Walton staged his first sales promotion called the "remodeling sale," and then the following March he had the grand opening.

Wal-Mart first opened in 1962 and became the world's number one retailer. Wal-Mart's success has also given many people today an opportunity for a bigger job market. More than 600,000 Americans work at Wal-Mart. The reason for its popular success is that it still follows Sam Walton's values: By hometown identity, each person is welcomed personally by People Greeters; each store honors a graduating high school senior with a college scholarship bake sales to benefit a local charity; associates determine where charitable funds are donated; the prices are low, and customers do not have to wait for a sale to see savings.

This is only to name a few of the things that Wal-Mart does for the community. Wal-Mart goes according to what Sam Walton believed: "Each Wal-Mart store should reflect the values of its customers and support the vision they hold for their community."

The Program(s)

Wal-Mart's Scholarships

Nationwide. Wal-Mart Associate Scholarship. A $1,000 scholarship offered to high school seniors who work for Wal-Mart Stores, Inc., and to those associates' children ineligible for the Walton Foundation Scholarship (due to parents length of employment or not working full time). Applications must be postmarked to Wal-Mart Foundation no later than March 1.

Distribution Center Scholarship. Two $2,500 scholarships payable over four years will be awarded in each unit that has been operating for one year as of May 1. Only associates who work at these Distribution Centers are eligible for this scholarship. Applications are available through the Distribution personnel manager beginning in January with May being the deadline. The basic criterion for a Distribution Center associate to be eligible for consideration is to have worked 1,000 hours as of May 1.

The Sam Walton Community Scholarship. Wal-Mart established the Sam Walton Community Scholarship Program in 1981. With this program, a $1,000 college scholarship is available to a local high school senior by each Wal-Mart store. This money can be used toward the student's first-year tuition, books, or on-campus room and board. More than 2,300 scholarships are given annually. Each Wal-Mart store distributes applications to high school counselors in January.

Community Scholarships. Giving back to a diversed associate and customer community is very important at Wal-Mart. As the nation's largest employer of Hispanics and African Americans, Wal-Mart works with several national organizations to help qualified students of color which include The College Fund/UNCF; Thurgood Marshall Scholarship Fund, League of United Latin American Citizens, and University of Texas Pan-American.

♦ ♦ ♦

References

Arkansas. *World book encyclopedia.* (1994 ed.).

Smith, R., & Vance, S. (1994). *A history of Sam Walton's retail phenomenon.* New York: Twayne.

Website

http://www.walmartfoundation.org/students.html.

CHAPTER 3

The State: California

The state of California is the third largest state in the United States. According to the 1990 census, California had 29,760,021 inhabitants. Whites make up 69 percent of the population and blacks, 7.4 percent; additional population groups include 731,685 people of Filipino origin; 704,850 people of Chinese origin; 312,989 people of Japanese origin, 280,223 people of Vietnamese origin; 259,941 people of Korean origin; and 236,078 Native Americans. The original inhabitants of California comprised of 105 tribes and spoke the dialects of six linguistic families.

By the mid- 1990s California had a larger population than any other state and was the leading producer by value of both agricultural and manufactured goods. The word **California** is derived from the name of an imaginary island in a popular Spanish romance of the time. California is called the Golden State because of the importance of the gold rush in 1849 in the state's history.

California, one of the Pacific Coast states of the United States, entered the Union on September 9, 1850 as the thirty-first state. Agriculture and mining have always been important to the economy of California.

The capital is Sacramento. The state's bird is the California valley quail; the state flower, golden poppy; the state tree, California redwood; and the state song "I Love California."

The Person(s)

Mrs. Mary Catherine Swanson

San Diego. Mrs. Mary Catherine Swanson is known throughout professional circles as a hardworking, dedicated individual. She taught high school English for 20 years before moving to the San Diego County Office of Education. As an English teacher, she demanded nothing short of excellence from her students—having worked with them individually to help them reach their maximum. Her students were active in many contests and other kinds of literary works. During that time she was instrumental in developing numerous award-winning language arts programs. In 1980 she developed AVID (Advancement Via Individual Determination), a secondary school program which prepares underachieving students for four-year college entry. More than 93 percent of AVID students enroll in college.

Among the awards and recognitions Mrs. Swanson has received are the A+ Award for Reaching the Goals of America 2000 from the United States Department of Education, EXCEL Award for Excellence in Teaching, Salute to Excellence from the American Association for Higher Education, and Headliner of the Year from the San Diego Press Club.

Additional accolades include: Listed in Who's Who in America and was the commencement speaker at San Diego State University in 1992; the only public school teacher ever to have won the $50,000 award for Pioneering Achievement in Education from the Charles A. Dana Foundation in New York.

In presenting the award, the Dana Foundation cited her for "heeding the teacher's calling at the highest level of professional dedication in developing AVID, an imaginative restructuring of the school day that has given thousands of students the skills, support and guidance that they need to fulfill their potential to prepare for a college education."

CALIFORNIA

The Program(s)

Streetcats Foundation

Los Angeles. **Streetcats Foundation** began working with street kids, runaways, and other at-risk youth on the streets of New York, Philadelphia, Los Angeles, and San Francisco in 1988. It became a non-profit corporation in 1991, a tax-exempt 501c3 organization, and California public benefit corporation in early 1993.

Over the years, Streetcats, with its familiar blue-and-yellow jeeps, worked miracles on city streets, getting teens and young adult victims of abuse that other counselors, police and probation officers had give up on, off alcohol and other drugs, reconciled with loved ones and into productive lives. Through time, patience, and tough love, the Streetcast program worked! The Streetcats program is a model for other cities.

Streetcats Foundation now sponsors the annual national Kids N' Need radio-thons (beginning in 1996), produces the national radio public service announcement advocacy series "Through the Eyes of a Child," administers the National Children's Coalition (an educational and membership organization for children and youth workers and advocates and their organizations) and produces the content for the new Internet World Wide Website.

The California Mentor Teacher Program

Statewide. **The California Mentor Teacher Program** was established in 1983 by Senate Bill 813. According to the law, the intent of the Mentor Teacher Program is to "encourage teachers currently employed in the public school system to continue to pursue excellence within their profession, to provide incentives for teachers of demonstrated ability and expertise to remain in the public school system, and to restore the teaching profession to its position of primary importance within the structure of the educational system."

California Migrant Education Literature Project (CAMEL)

Statewide. The project entails a four-week summer institute student academy at California State University, Dominguez Hills, California State University, Northridge and California Polytechnic University at Pomona. Students study literature-based lessons where the processes of active learning in heterogeneous groups involve them in challenging, collaborative language arts projects, which are the mainstay of instruction. Students participate in follow-up activities throughout the year, which culminate with a reunion the following summer. The mission is to help students focus on reading in the content areas and address reading, writing, and listening skills development through selected literature.

DIAL III Standardization: Migrant Preschool Program

Statewide. This is a voluntary assessment project for children ages 2 years 5 months to 5 years 5 months to measure a child's general developmental level. This is also used for screening potentially delayed children who need professional evaluation.

Implemented in collaboration with American Guidance Services, Circle Pines, Minnesota, the project collects data and distributes this information to the standardization data pool on the migrant education preschool population as part of a revision of the DIAL (Development Indicators for the Assessment of Learning), to be called DIAL III, in both English and Spanish. The Migrant Education Preschool program's participants in 14 districts are targeted and approximately 98 percent of those participating are Spanish speaking, a group that was underrepresented in previous standardizations.

CALIFORNIA 17

♦ ♦ ♦

References

California. *World book encyclopedia.* (1998 ed.).

Streetcats Foundation, 267 Lester Avenue, Suite 104, Oakland, California 94606.

CHAPTER 4

The State: Connecticut

The state of Connecticut derived its name from an Algonquian term probably meaning "place of the long river," referring to. It entered the union on January 9, 1788 as the fifth of the original 13 states. Connecticut is a producer of aircraft engines, helicopters, submarines, and firearms.

On one hand, Connecticut is serene and gracious, seemingly so unmarred by time that to see Nathan Hale stride across a local green would cause no surprise. On the other hand, there are clamorous manufacturing cities like Bridgeport and Hartford.

According to the 1990 census, Connecticut had 3,284,116 inhabitants. Whites make up 87 percent of the population and blacks 8.3; additional groups include 11,755 people of Indian origin, 11,082 people of Chinese origin, 6,472 Native Americans, 5,160 people of Filipino origin, and 5,126 people of Korean origin.

Connecticut is home to a wide variety of cultural institutions, including the oldest free public art museum in the United States—the Wadsworth Atheneum (1842). Eli Whitney, a Connecticut resident, developed the cotton gin.

The capital is Hartford. The state bird is the American robin; the state tree, the charter oak; and the state flower, mountain laurel.

The Person(s)

Mrs. Paula Brown Edme

Nationwide. Mrs. Paula Brown Edme is an African American who works hard to promote equality for all of humanity as well as coordinating several programs. Upon graduation from college she taught in the New York City Public School System.

She presently holds the position of Director of the Northeast Region of the NAACP since April 1986. Her duties include coordinating the activities and programs of branches and youth units in Connecticut, Delaware, New Hampshire, Maine, Massachusetts, Rhode Island, Vermont, New Jersey, New York, Pennsylvania, and Germany. Recently added to her area of concentration were the states of Virginia, Maryland, and the District of Columbia.

Further, she assists branches in improving the political, educational, social, and economic status of African Americans by eliminating racial prejudice and discrimination, in all of society. In addition, she is responsible for building the membership base of the NAACP and raising funds to support its program.

In her current position as the regional director, she is also responsible for working with NAACP youth councils and college chapters throughout the region. This affords her the opportunity to meet and speak with young people frequently. She assists NAACP youth with issues that confront them on a day-to-day basis and implement the programs of the NAACP. Through motivation and positive direction, she helps to develop leadership skills in young people that are necessary for them to take their rightful place as our future leaders.

Prior to Mrs. Edme's promotion, she served as acting National Director of the NAACP Youth and College Division; Regional Youth Director, and Regional Youth Director for six years.

CONNECTICUT

The Program(s)

Waterbury Community Release Program

Waterbury. This 28-bed program serves both male and female clients referred by the State of Connecticut Department of Correction. In this program, clients are afforded the opportunity to establish vocational and educational skills, support system, and independent living skills prior to entering the community. All of this is accomplished through a two-phase system.

The first phase consists of a 30-day intensive program that is geared toward assisting clients in recognizing and addressing issues regarding institutionalization, program structure, regulations, client goals, vocational/educational opportunities, individual and group therapy, 12-step self-help programs, AIDS education, basic health issues, recreational therapy, and family systems re-establishment. During this phase, community access is available only with a staff escort.

Once clients have received a positive evaluation from staff, they enter the second phase. This phase consists of a 90- to 120-day work release program. During this phase each client secures employment and continues to attend group and individual counseling as well as self-help group meetings. Completion of the program is based on the client's participation level, employment, securing of appropriate residence, aftercare planning and legal status.

Referrals are accepted only from the State of Connecticut Department of Correction.

For more information contact Mr. Mark Yates, Director of Waterbury Residential Programs, Waterbury Community Release Program, 31 Wolcott Street, Waterbury, Connecticut.

◆ ◆ ◆

References

Connecticut. *World book encyclopedia*. (1998 ed.).

Yates, Mark, Director of Waterbury Residential Programs, Waterbury Community Release Program, 31 Wolcott Street, Waterbury, Connecticul 06702.

Website

http://www.local.naacp.org/eframe

CHAPTER 5

The State: Delaware

The state of Delaware is the second smallest state of the United States, next to Rhode Island. It is known as **The First State** because on December 7, 1787, it became the first state to ratify the United States Constitution. Delaware lies close to many of the nation's largest industrial cities. It is the only state in which counties are divided into areas called hundreds.

Delaware inhabited people from Dutch, Swedish, and English backgrounds during the 1600s. According to the 1990 census, Delaware had 666,168 inhabitants. Whites accounted for 80.3 percent of the population and blacks 16.9 percent; additional population groups included 2,301 people of Chinese descent; 2,183 people of Asian Indian background; and 1,982 Native Americans. Nearly 16,000 people were of Hispanic ancestry. Methodists and Roman Catholics were the leading groups in Delaware.

Delaware has humid climate with hot summers and mild winters. Services and industries account for 65 percent of Delaware's gross state products.

Delaware contains about 3,000 farms. The state is a major U. S. producer of broiler chickens and poultry products, and also supplies dairy items and potatoes and other vegetables for sale in nearby cities.

The capital is Dover. The state bird is the blue hen chicken; the state tree, American holly; and the state flower, peach blossom.

The Person(s)

Ms. Marianne Locke

Dover City. Ms. Marianne Locke is a Caucasian American who received a Bachelor of Music degree from Northwestern University and a Master of Arts in education from the University of California at Berkeley. On the verge of pursuing a doctorate in educational leadership, she is a lifelong student and educator.

Ms. Locke is the Executive Director of the American Conservator Theater in Dover City, Delaware. In the city of Dover, there are various ethnic groups which include Caucasians, African Americans, and Asians.

She has taught for over 11 years in various school districts and is the founder and director of a private school. Since she became director of Young Imaginations in 1988, Ms. Locke has continued to teach music classes as part of a Young Imaginations school program which emphasizes community partnerships.

She acts as an active presenter at workshops and clinics at Delaware's state level conferences and at universities nationwide. She has served as the multicultural representative on the Board of the California Music Educators Association since 1991. She has produced **Voices of the World**, an annual cross-cultural concert series. Additionally, she acts as coordinator/designer for local school programs working with numerous artists and performing groups. Her love for music of various kinds allowed her to co-author **Being in Motion**, a teacher handbook, video, and music CD, **Everybody's Welcome** songs and singing games for grades K-3, **The Way West** which includes songs and dances for grades 4-8, and **The Magic of Music**, a beginning instrumental and music reading series for grades 4-8.

Ms. Locke has made an indelible contribution to society with her sharing and love for music with the kids.

The Program(s)

Jersey Cape Dance Center

Statewide. What began as a school project has turned into a statewide activity that allows students to share through dance their interpretation of the Holocaust.

After having the experience of hearing and being personally moved by the Sam Harris song "Suffer the Innocent" on the radio, Stina Smith decided she wanted to use music to motivate and educate her dance group. Her research included visiting the United States Memorial Holocaust Museum in Washington, D.C., interviewing women and children of the Holocaust (which she received their diaries). This visit proved very worthy in that Ms. Smith sparked her students' interests and they became curious and wanted to know more about the Holocaust.

After sharing her research with her students, Ms. Smith required her students to role-play by writing a first person essay describing what it would be like to be taken from their homes, separated from their families, and put into concentration camps. "The piece starts as if they are getting herded off of a train, and I wanted them to understand what they had left behind, and what had happened to get them up to this point," says Smith. "In these essays, I was so impressed that they had absorbed so much from the dance."

As a result of this assignment, Jersey Cape Dance Center Stina Smith has created a dance about the Holocaust. In fact, the costumes are modeled after prisoners' uniforms she viewed on the National Holocaust Museum. Ms. Smith received such raved reviews from audiences that she decided to enter **Suffer the Innocent** into a convention competition, in which entries rarely cover subjects so weighty. Instead of the usual laughter, whooping, and hollering, the audience was moved to tears and silence. Ms. Smith says that to see such a serious audience was an experience in itself.

♦ ♦ ♦
References

Delaware. *World book encyclopedia*. (1999 ed.).

Sims, C. (1997, November). Teaching history through dance. *Dance*, pp. 72-73.

Website

http://www.youngimaginations.org/

CHAPTER 6

The State: Florida

The state of Florida is one of the leading tourist states in the nation. This land of swaying palm trees and warm ocean breezes attracts visitors throughout the year, usually about 40 million annually. It entered the union on March 3, 1845 as the twenty-seventh state.

According to the 1990 census, Florida had 12,937,926 inhabitants. Whites make up 83.1 percent of the population and blacks, 13,6 percent. Additional population groups include 35,461 Native Americans, 31,457 people of Indian origin, 31, 945 people of Filipino origin, 30,737 people of Chinese origin, 16,346 people of Vietnamese origin, 12,404 people of Korean origin, and 8,505 people of Japanese origin.

Florida has been nicknamed the **Sunshine State** because of its large number of sunny days. The state's nickname reflects the economic importance of its climate, which has been called its most important natural resource. Among the other nicknames, all unofficial, are the **Everglade State** and the **Orange State**, for its most renowned crop. Many older persons spend their retirement years in the state. Miami Beach, a suburb of Miami, is one of the world's most famous resort centers.

The capital is Tallahassee. The state bird is the mockingbird; the state tree, sabal palmetto palm; and the state flower, orange blossom.

The Person(s)

Mrs. Ethel Koger Beckham

Miami. With her motto "Nurturing Every Child's Potential," Mrs. Ethel Koger Beckham is known to many as a "born educator." She was born in Paducah, Kentucky and moved to Miami in 1923. She attended Dade County Public Schools from Kindergarten at Riverside Elementary through her graduation from Miami High in 1937.

She met Walter Beckham in junior high at Ada Merrit and marched with him in graduation from Miami High. They married during the war and had three children.

After serving in volunteer work in the community for years, Mrs. Beckham ran for the School Board in 1968. She served 16 years on the School Board and loved every minute of it. She said that it seemed everything she had ever learned prepared her for the job. She took office at the time of the statewide teacher strike, and then experienced court ordered desegregation. Those were turbulent times for the community.

Her other professional affiliations included: President on the Florida School Board's Association, as well as the Southern Region of the National Board's Association. She served on state boards in various capacities, and was appointed on the Board of National Career Education in Washington, D.C.

The school, named after her—Ethel Koger Beckham Elementary, has as its mission state "Every child comes to school with strengths and abilities." Mrs. Beckham believes in project-based learning, portfolio assessment, performance-based standards, collaborative efforts, a blend of new and traditional approaches, and technological practices to achieve these goals.

The staff of Ethel Koger Beckham Elementary School is committed to connect these abilities with deeper and wider ways of knowing, finding the intelligence, building character within all students, seeing each child as an individual with unique hopes, dreams, skills, and needs.

The Program(s)

North Dade Center for Modern Languages

Miami. "Preparing Global Thinkers for a Multicultural World" is the motto for North Dade Center for Modern Languages. The North Dade Center for Modern Languages is a magnet school that has a reputation for excellence nationwide and locally. It has received the high honor of being named a Blue Ribbon School of Excellence by the President and the United States Department of Education in 1992. Other acknowledgements include **Redbook's** "America's Best Schools" (1995); "Art in Public Places" (1996); and Magnet Schools of America's "Magnets School of Merit" (1997).

The Center for Modern Languages provides an opportunity for qualified elementary school students living in the north end of Miami-Dade County to study to become multilingual and multicultural; receive two/three hours daily of French or Spanish instruction; participate in a challenging academic program; attend early bird foreign language classes; participate in a home-based gifted center for qualified students; communicate with the world through telecommunications; participate in a Cooperative Agreement Educational Program with the Spanish government in grades 3-5; and experience an extended elementary school day (8:30-3:00 grade 1 and 8:30-4:00 grades 2-5).

The professional team at North Dade Center for Modern Languages has made a commitment to prepare its students for the challenges ahead by providing an education which builds upon the basic skills foundation. By encouraging creativity and promoting analytical and reflective thinking, it is hoped that future citizens will acquire multicultural experiences and show a mutual respect on the road to becoming bilingual, biliterate critical thinkers.

Communities In Schools

Statewide. Through strategic community partnerships, **Communities In Schools (CIS)** brings private and public resources into schools to help at-risk youth improve their attendance, grades, and social development. Services include academic tutoring, mentoring, social and career skills building, scholarships, case management, and supportive counseling for students and their families.

Founded in 1977, Communities In Schools is today the nation's largest stay-in-school network. Communities In Schools brings together hands in need with hands that can help. By relocating community service providers to work as a personalized team serving alongside teachers, principals, volunteers, and mentors, CIS connects the schools with the resources that students need most.

Millions of young people have lost the traditional safety nets that used to provide love and security even when the nuclear family was in trouble. Extended families, close-knit neighborhoods, a church, a synagogue or mosque all could be counted on to respond when these kids cried out for help. But now, the safety net is too often stretched to the breaking point.

Projects offered through CIS include:
- **Learning Buddies** are volunteers recruited from local colleges and businesses to tutor CIS students primarily in reading and math.
- **Families and Schools Together (FAST)** efforts offer adult members of CIS families occasions to join together in parent education and training.
- **Youth Leadership Broward** participants are eleventh graders in the Leadership Broward Foundation's year long leadership development program.
- **FSU Summer Experience** gathers CIS students from across Florida to spend two weeks living in a dorm and attending classes.
- **Student Incentive Program** rewards CIS students for improved grades, attendance, and behavior with individualized student incentives.

♦ ♦ ♦

References

Communities In Schools of Broward County, Incorporated, 4790 N. State Road 7, Suite 200, Fort Lauderdale, Florida.

Florida. *World book encyclopedia.* (1998 ed.).

The Center for Modern Languages, 1840 NW 157 Street, Miami, Florida.

CHAPTER 7

The State: Georgia

The state of Georgia has a larger area than any other state east of the Mississippi River. It entered the union on January 2, 1788 as the fourth state. Georgia is named for George II of Great Britain and Ireland, and is known as the Empire State of the South.

According to the 1990 census, Georgia had 6,478,216 inhabitants. Whites make up 71 percent of the population and blacks, 27 percent; other groups include 15,275 people of Korean origin, 13,926 people of Indian origin, 12,926 Native Americans, and 12,657 persons of Chinese origin. About 109,000 people are of Hispanic origin.

Jimmy Carter became the first native Georgian to win election to the U. S. presidency. Dr. Martin Luther King, Jr., was the first Georgian to win the Nobel Peace Prize. Eli Whitney invented the cotton gin on a Georgia plantation. Atlanta and Georgia hosted the 1966 Centennial Olympic Games. John Wesley founded America's first Protestant Sunday School in Savannah. America's first gold rush began at Auraria, Lumpkin County, near Dahlonega. Juliette Gordon Low established the Girl Scouts of the USA in Savannah. Rebecca Felton of Cartersville became the first woman in the U. S. Senate. Former Republican Speaker of the House Newt Gingrich is from Georgia.

The capital is Atlanta. The state bird is the brown thrasher; the state crop, the peanut; the state fruit, the peach; and the state flower, Cherokee rose.

The Person(s)

Rev. Rosa Arnold

Atlanta. There are undoubtedly many people in Atlanta volunteering their time, money, and efforts to troubled, abused, and neglected children throughout the area, but there is one particular woman that stands out and her name is Rev. Rosa Arnold.

Just recently Rev. Arnold, an African American, and seven other women were awarded the "Eckerd 100 Symposium: A Salute to Women." Rev. Arnold started her mission for helping young children after a tragic accident touched her own life. Her son was killed in 1996 while working on a part-time job. This tragedy made Rev. Arnold want to do something about children who live in drug addicted and abused homes. She opened the Albert T. Mills Center in honor of her son.

The Albert T. Mills Center is located in downtown Atlanta. The Center mainly focuses on preschoolers who have drug addicted parents.

The Hit Man of Atlanta

Atlanta. When Jermaine Dupri, now 25 and the hottest producer in rhythm and blues, was just a teen, he discovered, designed, and launched the kiddie rap group Kris Kross. The group consists of two African Americans in their early teens who do rap music. The duet has appeared on television numerous times and won several awards.

Meanwhile, Dupri himself remains a very private person. He likes to be self-contained, to have everything he wants, everything he needs, everything he cares about close at hand; in fact, so close, as within the walls of his airy Atlanta home. Often when staff members at the record company hold meetings, Dupri does not even leave his house to attend, but calls in via speaker phone. He says "everybody else got kids, families. It's completely music for me."

The Program(s)

Tickets for Kids

Atlanta. Atlanta has many fun and exciting things for kids to see and do such as Six Flags Over Georgia, The Coca-Cola Factory, the Underground Mall, and the Martin Luther King, Jr., attractions. Kids can visit most of these attractions just for being kids or while on vacation. But there is a program in Atlanta that rewards kids for their outstanding efforts in their community called **Tickets for Kids.**

What this program does is reward kids for contributions that they make in their community by giving them tickets to sporting events, concerts, and performing arts. **Tickets for Kids** is a unified effort of Ticketmaster-Southeast and Atlanta Mayor Bill Campbell to channel family entertainment tickets as rewards and incentives to youth who have proven the willingness to contribute to their community. Nationally, the programs are located through the United States in 18 cities from the east coast to the west coast. These cities include: Charlotte, Chicago, Cleveland, Dallas, Detroit, Los Angeles, Kansas City, Missouri, Kansas City, Kansas, Memphis, Minneapolis, Orlando, Philadelphia, Raleigh, San Diego, Seattle, and St. Paul.

Camp Sunshine

Atlanta. Children with cancer often feel isolated, deserted, and unable to share their pain and innermost thoughts. Founded in 1983, a summer camp was developed for children with cancer. Children who attend Camp Sunshine counsel, play, pray, and live together. The programs have brought hope, support, and love to children with cancer and their families. Camp Sunshine has grown from a one-week program to a year-round program serving hundreds of children annually.

References

Georgia. *World book encyclopedia*. (1998 ed.).

The City of Atlanta, Mayor's Office of Community Affairs, Atlanta, Georgia.

Scott, P. (1998, October). Atlanta women are honored as volunteers. *The Atlanta Constitution*.

Staunton, M. (1991). Young students learning library. New York: Funk & Wagnalls, Incorporated.

Farley, C. (1998, July). The hit man of Atlanta. *Time*, 152 (3).

Website

http://www.wbmaster@ci.atlanta.ga.us

http://www.campsunshine.com

CHAPTER 8

The State: Hawaii

The state of Hawaii has a nickname of **Aloha,** which is used for both greeting and farewell in the Hawaiian language. It is the fiftieth state to be admitted to the union on August 21, 1959.

According to the 1990 census, Hawaii had 1,108,229 inhabitants. Whites constitute 33.4 percent of the population, the lowest proportion of any state; blacks constitute 2.5 percent of the total. Among the many other population groups are 247,486 people of Japanese origin; 168,682 people of Filipino origin; 138,742 people of Hawaiian origin; 68,804 people of Chinese origin; 24,454 people of Korean origin; and 15,034 people of Samoan origin. Many residents are of mixed race or ethnicity.

Hawaii is a very unique state. It is the only state in the United States that does not connect any other states. Hawaii is made up of islands. Hawaii is mostly known for its beauty and climate. Some islands included in the state of Hawaii are Hawaii, Maui, Oahu, Kauai, Molokai, Lanai, and Nihau. The highest point in Hawaii is the Mauna Kea, on the island of Hawaii. The lowest is sea level. Hawaii's climate is subtropical--its temperatures ranging from a historic high of about 100 F to a historic low of about 14 F.

The capital is Honolulu. The state bird is nene/Hawaiian goose; the state tree, kukui; and the state flower, yellow hibiscus.

The Person(s)

Rev. Lafete Tucker, Sr.

Oahu. Rev. Lafete Tucker, Sr., an African American, is the kind of person everyone should have as a friend. He is actively involved in helping the community by making positive things happen in the field of education, counseling, and sports in the city of Oahu. In the field of education, he works through his civic organization, Citizens for a Better Oahu, Inc., by tutoring students and assisting young adults in achieving their educational goals. In counseling, he works through his non-profit business, Tucker's Career Counseling Center, Inc., to give career awareness to young people in high school so that they may make wise decisions regarding their career goals. In sports, he is the President of the Oahu Area Bitty Basketball Association. Through the Association, he gives guidance to children ranging in ages from 5-13 an opportunity to better their awareness of teamwork.

The death of his brother is what motivated Rev. Tucker to do positive things for others. He grew up as a military kid and was always moving from one army base to another. He received a bachelor's degree in business management from the University of Texas at Austin and currently serves as pastor of the Mount Olive Baptist Church in Oahu, Hawaii. He also served on the city's local planning and zoning board. He and his wife Joyce are the proud parents of Heather and Lafete, Jr. They reside in Oahu.

Ms. Jane Campbell

Statewide. Ms. Jane Campbell is a producer of the Honolulu Theatre for Youth. She has been running the theatre along with others since the 1960s. The program is a non-profit business that involves young children in educational programs. She is responsible for getting the support, transportation, and sponsors.

The Program(s)

Speaking, Relating, and Learning

Honolulu. This program is a study of how well children learn at home or school. It started in 1996. The main focus of this program is to get children educated at home instead of school. The program is not trying to take away from the school system; instead to incorporate the same things at home. It is being used throughout Honolulu, Hawaii. It makes a big difference on where the program is being implemented. For example, Hawaii is a large state that exists with several small islands. Honolulu is the largest island in Hawaii and is where most civilization is located; but on other islands schools are very rare. So if a child lived on a small island, he/she might not get an education for several reasons.

One reason is that a school is not near. Another reason is that there is no information or help to give the parents in educating their youth. Next, many do not have money and transportation to get an education system. The goal of the **Speaking, Relating, and Learning Program** is to get every child in Hawaii educated. So far, the program has reached 65 percent of its goal.

The plan is really simple: Every parent is mailed an education package in which the parent can sign his child up for this program. Once the parent accepts, the parent is mailed rules and guidelines for the program. The child and surrounding neighbors must meet at least twice a week to share and quiz one another. The representative of the program mails the child learning assignments and booklets for the children to complete and return. Every six weeks students will meet with local representatives of the program to be evaluated.

The residents are very excited and look forward to meeting with representatives, fellowshipping with one another, and participating in the program.

Indigenous Language Immersion Programs

Statewide. Indigenous Language Immersion Programs are designed to bring back native language use in schools via immersion education. Five programs are highlighted in the article, yet the primary focus is on the Paphana Kaiapuni Program in the state of Hawaii. The purpose of each program in one way or another is to implement the total or partial inclusion of native languages into the school's curriculum.

Papahana Kaiapuni is a Hawaiian language immersion program that involves 1,100 students and 60 teachers in Kaiapuni schools on the islands of Oahu, Hawaii, Kauai, Maui, and Moloka in the state of Hawaii. The program began in 1987, emerging from an awakening that the Hawaiian language was beginning to disappear. The language had been banned from the schools for almost a century and one generation had already been deprived of its native language. After the realization that only the elderly speakers of the native Hawaiian were still alive, though few in number, the immediate emergence of the re-speaking of this language sparked the community.

The program is implemented in the public schools in Hawaii for K-12 grades. Because of parents, activists and Hawaiian educators being actively involved in the Kaiapuni program, the curriculum in schools is followed in the Hawaiian language. Students begin receiving English instruction once they excel to the fifth grade; only an hour of English is introduced everyday. Some schools provide English instruction in Hawaiian language while others teach English through English immersion. The controversy surrounding the use of English in Kaiapuni classrooms is an example of the multiculturalism being reflected via educators and parental involvement.

The goals of the Kaiapuni program are to develop a high level of proficiency in comprehension and communication in the Hawaiian language, develop a strong Hawaiian culture foundation, and develop knowledge and skills in all areas of the curriculum so that the students may become responsible and caring individuals throughout the communities in Hawaii.

◆ ◆ ◆
References

Boggs, S., McMillen, G., & Watson-Gegeo, K. (1995). *Studies of Hawaii children*. United States: Ablex.

Fergusson, E. (1995). *Our Hawaii*. New York: Alfred A. Knopf.

Hawaii. *World book encyclopedia*. (1998 ed.).

Interview. Rev. Lefete Tucker, Sr., November 17, 1998. Hammond, Louisiana.

Yamauchi, L. & Ceppi, A. (1998). A review of indigenous language immersion programs and a focus on Hawaii. *Equity and Excellence in Education, 31,* 11-19.

Website

http://www.openstudio.hawaii.edu/hty/Jane.html

http://www.openstudio.hawaii.edu/hty/welcome.html

CHAPTER 9

The State: Idaho

The state of Idaho is a rocky mountain state with exciting scenery. It entered the union on July 3, 1890 as the forty-third state. Idaho's nickname is the **Gem State**, for Gem of the Mountains.

According to the 1990 census, Idaho had 1,006,749 inhabitants. Whites make up 94.4 percent of the population and blacks, 0.3 percent; additional population groups include 13,594 Native Americans and 2,719 people of Japanese origin. About 52,900 people are of Hispanic, mainly Mexican origin. Among the principal Native American groups are the Nez Perce and Shoshone. Half of the people in Idaho live in cities and towns. Many residents are descendants of early English, Irish, and Scottish settlers from the Eastern and Midwestern states. Mormons make up the largest single religious group in Idaho. Other large denominations in the state include Roman Catholics, Methodists, Lutherans, Episcopalians, and Presbyterians.

Idaho farmers grow sugar, beets, wheat, and many other crops. But Idaho's most famous produce are potatoes. Idaho ranks first among the states in potato production, and people throughout the United States enjoy Idaho's baked potatoes.

The capital is Boise. The state bird is the mountain bluebird and the state tree is the western white pine.

The Person(s)

Dr. Marilyn Howard

Statewide. Dr. Marilyn Howard, a Caucasian female, is the superintendent of Public Instruction in Idaho. She grew up in Mackey, Idaho where she attended school. She received her bachelor's degree in education and a Master of Science degree from the University of Idaho. Later, she obtained a Doctor of Education in Curriculum and Education Science from Brigham Young University. She has worked at Idaho State University and the University of Idaho as an adjunct faculty member in reading and language arts.

Dr. Howard started teaching in 1960 in Lewiston where she taught high school history and language. She continued teaching at the elementary and secondary schools in Idaho and Washington. Twenty eight years later she became principal at a Developmental Preschool for Moscow School District. Her last and most recent accomplishment was her promotion to superintendent of Public Instruction in Idaho, January, 1999.

She has contributed to the community by aiding in the accreditation team evaluations of teacher education programs throughout the state of Idaho. She continues her research and publication career with the goal of helping all students with their reading comprehension skills.

Her professional activities include:
- State coordinator and state president of the International Reading Association
- Member of the Association's National Research and Studies Committee
- Member of accreditation teams for evaluating teacher education programs in Idaho

Dr. Howard continues on a daily basis to strive and maintain excellence through her on-going research and working with the individual schools in her district.

Dr. Vincent Muli Wa Kituku

Boise. Dr. Vincent Muli Wa Kituku, an African, is an academician and business professional who speaks from worldwide experience--nurturing the human spirit and culture. He resides in Boise, Idaho. He is a native of Kenya, Africa. He earned a Doctor of Philosophy degree in range management from the University of Wyoming in 1991.

Dr. Kituku is a former training specialist with Idaho Power Company and active adjunct professor at Boise State University. He is a motivational speaker and storyteller. He is also a columnist for weekly and monthly newspapers for more than ten newspapers in Idaho, Texas, and Oregon. His articles also appear in *Creative Training* regularly. Dr. Kituku has a weekly radio program called **Buffaloes in Our Lives**.

He does school presentations, such as African folktales, wildlife, and culture. Students are given an in-dept overview of Africa's geography, culture, tradition, conservation methods, and interaction with the western cultures. Dr. Kituku's warm enthusiasm and engaging style creates an excellent rapport with students. The presentation interactively uses slides, African artifacts such as wood carvings, crafts, and traditional spear and other African props. Riveting African folktales and students' participation make these presentations not only educational, but entertaining and memorable.

The folktales in particular are thought-provoking, inclusive, and informative. Using them, students analyze life lessons such as

- Staying away from destructive substances
- Character, positive self image
- Respect for elders, sharing
- Making healthy decisions
- Setting goals and work ethics

Dr. Kituku is a dynamic and award-winning speaker. He has helped thousands of people. He believes that each individual has an "amazing grace" to sing.

The Program(s)

Individualized Education Programs

Statewide. Public Law 94-142 Individuals with Disabilities Education Act (IDEA) states that an Individualized Education Program (IEP) must be developed for each student found eligible for special education and/or related services. An Individual Education Program (IEP) is a written document which outlines the plan developed to meet the unique needs and enhances the strengths of an individual student.

Each student's IEP defines the special program and related services that will be provided to an individual student. The IEP is developed by a group of experts called a Child Study Team and is reviewed at least annually. The members responsible for developing each student's IEP are the student's parents, the student when appropriate, special and/or regular education teachers, an administrator, and others such as therapists, psychologists, etc.

Parents can make a real contribution to the design of their child's educational program when they take some time to think about the goals that they would like to see their child reach. It is important to determine appropriately an IEP by the student's strengths and weaknesses.

Objectives must be developed. Objectives are the tasks or steps the child will need to complete to master the goal. (A goal is a skill or behavior). The objectives should be written so that the parent and the school can see and measure the steps to meet the goals and spell out the criteria that the Child Study Team feels the student must meet before the objectives will be deemed completed.

Idaho has implemented a voluntary mediation system under which families and schools can resolve their disagreements and potentially avoid due process. Both school and family voluntarily agree to meet to discuss and resolve their disagreements.

Helping Homeless Families

Boise. Boise is known for being the trade center for a large agricultural livestock-raising region of eastern Oregon and southwestern Idaho. What people do not know is that inside the city of Boise is a program designed to help the homeless regain their lives.

In 1989 a grant from the Better Homes Foundation (the nonprofit organization founded by *Better Homes and Gardens* magazine) was established to help homeless families find jobs and become independent. Donations from their readers have been instrumental in providing money for the foundation to distribute to local organizations that work with homeless families throughout the country. To date, the foundation has raised nearly $1.9 million.

The program does the following: First, the family provides a $50 deposit to get into a house that is provided by the organization. Then the Boise Neighborhood Housing Service provides the family with housing, counseling, and connections to support care systems such as daycare and health care for the next two years. Prior to the establishment of this program, homeless families in Boise were only provided with 60 days of temporary shelter.

The article focuses on a white family that met the necessary requirements. The mother of two was in an abusive marriage and decided to leave her husband. She went to a nearby shelter and was given information on this program. She worked for Boise Neighborhood housing to earn the $50 she needed for her deposit.

The mother had a typical profile of women from abusive families: A husband who drank and took his anger out on her and the children; a father who had a similar pattern with her mother—thereby putting her in this type of environment for most of her life; blame that children place on themselves as being the fault of not having a "normal" household.

The decision she made that day was the beginning of the first day of the rest of a productive, full life for her and her children.

♦ ♦ ♦

References

Daly, M. (1990, October). Helping homeless families. *Better Homes and Gardens*, pp. 15, 16.

Elbow, G., & Ludwig, G. (1991). People in time and place. Morristown: Silver Burdett and Ginn.

Idaho Parents Unlimited, Incorporated, Parent Education and Resource Center, 4696 Overland Road #478, Boise, Idaho.

Idaho. *World book encyclopedia*. (1994 ed.).

Kituku, V. (1999, Spring). Vincent Kituku's school program. *Buffaloes in Our Lives*, pp. 1-5.

McNally, R. (1993). Discovery atlas of the United States. United States: Rand McNally and Company.

Titone, J. (1998, Winter). A lesson for a lifetime. *American Forest*, p. 48.

Website

http://www.id.us.com

CHAPTER 10

The State: Illinois

The state of Illinois serves as the heart of America both geographically and culturally. It entered the union on December 3, 1818 as the twenty-first state. Chicago is the nation's third largest city.

Known as the **Land of Lincoln**, Illinois is often associated with Abraham Lincoln, who lived in the state for much of his life. The name of the state is taken from that of the Illinois, or Illini, Native American Confederation.

According to the 1990 census, Illinois had 11,430,602 inhabitants. Whites make up 78.3 percent of the population and blacks 14.8 percent. The number of Asians and Pacific Islanders rose by nearly 79 percent in the 1980s; they include 64,224 people of Filipino descent, 64,200 people of Indian origin, 49,936 people of Chinese origin, and 41,506 people of Korean origin. More than 900,000 residents are of Hispanic origin. There are 20,970 Native Americans. Polish Americans make up a significant minority in the Chicago area.

Many famous people are included in the history of Illinois: Industrialists Cyrus H. McCormick and George M. Pullman; writers Gwendolyn Brooks and Carl Sandburg; architects Louis Sullivan and Frank Lloyd Wright; reformers Jane Adams and Florence Kelly and political leader Stephen A. Douglas.

The capital is Springfield. The state bird is the cardinal; the state tree, white oak; and the state flower, native violet.

The Person(s)

Pastor James T. Meeks

Chicago. Pastor James T. Meeks, an African American, is one of America's most dynamic and inspirational spiritual leaders. He is the senior pastor of the Salem Baptist Church of Chicago. Pastor Meeks spends countless hours developing life-changing sermons that inspire his congregation and others to fully understand and fulfill their purpose in the Body of Christ. He is committed to developing mature believers who understand God's purpose for their life and are willing to live according to the Word of God.

Under his leadership, Salem Baptist Church of Chicago has grown from 205 members in 1985 to well over 9,000 in 1998. Salem's members are excited about learning and spreading the Word of God. This is evident in the fact that Salem has the largest Sunday School in the City of Chicago.

Under Pastor Meeks' direction, various ministries were organized at Salem, including an effective Prison Ministry, Feed the Homeless Program, which feeds local homeless individuals on a weekly basis, Substance Abuse Program; Children's Ministry, and a Youth Ministry. Salem also hosts several events throughout the year including Youth Conferences, Married Couples Retreats, Singles Summits, Children's Camping Trips, Church Growth Seminars, Christian Education Seminars, and Health and Wellness Workshops.

Out of concern for the quality of education children receive, Pastor Meeks established the Salem Christian Academy. The focus of the Academy is to educate children from nursery three-year-olds through eighth grade. In addition, he organized a mentoring program entitled **Just Do It** which is responsible for placing youth in direct contact with neighborhood leaders and church members who serve as role models to the young men and women.

Mr. Kirby Puckett

Chicago. Born on March 14, 1961, Mr. Kirby Puckett was the youngest of nine children. Growing up in Chicago, Illinois, he and his family lived in the Robert Taylor Homes, one of the most violent, gang infested housing projects.

As a young boy he would come home from school, do his homework and then look for other kids to play baseball. Once he became a teenager, he was plagued with shortness. At 5 feet 4 inches, he knew he would not get much taller so he decided to start lifting weights. He got stronger and faster and his game of baseball improved tremendously. As a senior in high school he was an All-American, which lead him to receive an athletic scholarship for baseball at Bradley University in Peoria, Illinois. Then his father died. So he transferred closer to home to Triton College. While at Triton College, the baseball team went to the Junior College World Series and that is where he got drafted. The Minnesota Twins drafted Mr. Puckett in 1982.

Unfortunately, Mr. Puckett is no longer playing baseball due to a sudden eye disease. He was diagnosed with glaucoma, which caused him to lose sight in his right eye. This is a "very serious disease that strikes without warning and disproportionately affects African Americans," states Mr. Puckett. What he didn't know was that glaucoma, a vicious disease, had sneaked upon him like a thief in the night and stole one of his most precious possessions. This is why he has undertaken a personal crusade. "I'm trying to make people aware, especially African Americans, that they need to get checked for glaucoma because I don't want what happened to me to happen to them," says Mr. Puckett, whose regular vision exams didn't include screening for glaucoma. "The only way that can be avoided is for people to take the first step, the ultimate step, and that is to get checked. Please take 10 to 15 minutes out of a day, go to your eye doctor and get checked for glaucoma because it doesn't give you any warning signs. It came, took the sight in my right eye, and I'll never be able to regain it," states Mr. Puckett. He states that his job is to make people aware of glaucoma.

The Program(s)

High Jump Program

Chicago. The Latin School of Chicago developed a High Jump Program. Since its inception in 1989, the mission of High Jump has been to prepare economically disadvantaged inner-city students of color with high academic potential to attend, and succeed at, selective college-preparatory high schools. This mission is accomplished by providing a challenging academic enrichment program in a nurturing environment. High Jump receives funding from the Lloyd A. Fry Foundation, corporations, other area foundations, and friends. Some additional facts about High Jump include:

- **Student Body.** Students enter High Jump after the sixth grade and remain with the program until high school. Over 220 students have participated in High Jump since its inception. Each class year of students is called a **Cohort**.
- **Academics.** The High Jump Program includes three years of intensive summer sessions and two years of Saturday programs during the school years of grades seventh and eighth.
- Key components of the High Jump curriculum are classes in math enrichment, language arts, computer technology, and social studies. Art, science, and public-speaking classes are included throughout the program.
- **Mini-Courses.** Afternoon sessions are dedicated to mini-courses, taught by volunteer Latin students and High Jump alumni. Mini-courses expose High Jump students to a variety of cultural, academic, and recreational subjects.
- **Facilities.** High Jump uses the campus of The Latin School for classes, athletics, and special events. The Latin School offers state-of-the-art technology, a 450-seat theatre, a 25-yard indoor swimming pool, and recently renovated and expanded classroom space.

♦ ♦ ♦
References

Chicago Sun-Times. (1998, July). City's liquor crackdown, p. 4A.

Illinois. *World book encyclopedia*. (1996 ed.).

Link Unlimited, 7759 S. Eberhart, Chicago, Illinois.

Salem Baptist Church of Chicago, 11800 S. Indiana Avenue, Chicago, Illinois.

The Christian Science Monitor. (1998, August). Just do it right, p. 7.

The Latin School of Chicago, 59 W. Boulevard, Chicago, Illinois.

CHAPTER 11

The State: Indiana

The state of Indiana is a small state with a large population. It entered the union on December 11, 1816 as the nineteenth state. Indiana is called the **Hossier State**, and its people are known as Hossiers.

According to the 1990 census, Indiana had 5,544,159 inhabitants. Whites made up 90.6 percent of the population and blacks, 7.8 percent; additional population groups included some 12,453 Native Americans, 7,371 people of Chinese origin, 7,095 Asian Indians, 5,475 people of Korean background, 4,754 people of Filipino ancestry, and 4,715 people of Japanese background. Nearly 100,000 Indiana residents were of Hispanic origin. Roman Catholics formed the single largest religious group in the state followed by the Baptist, Methodist, and Lutherans.

Indiana is one of the leading states in farming and manufacturing. Manufacturing is Indiana's chief source of income.

One of Indiana's famous towns is called, believe it or not, Santa Claus. The town of Santa Claus receives more than a half million packages, letters, and cards, during the Christmas season.

The capital is Indianapolis. The state bird is the cardinal; the state tree, tulip; and the state flower, peony.

The Person(s)

Mr. Chris Karimu

Indianapolis. Mr. Chris Karimu is a Caucasian and a resident of Indianapolis, Indiana. He has served as Executive Director of Flanner House in Indianapolis since 1992.

Flanner House is a charitable organization which began in 1898 when Frank Flanner, a local philanthropist and Caucasian mortician, donated two frame buildings to the Charity Organization with instructions to create a Negro Community Service Center. Since its inception, Flanner House has demonstrated its commitment to the provision of human services by planning and implementing a variety of employment and training, social services, recreational, and health programs. The agency's programs have always been aided by the cooperative efforts of individuals in the community. Programs include a recreation department with boys and girls clubs; vocational arts with classes in cooking, sewing and millinery; a music department with a full orchestra of 73 pieces; and a daycare nursery that charge ten cents a day.

Mr. Karimu's accomplishments include:
- Healthy Baby Program
- Purdue University and Indiana University research projects
- HUD child care expansion
- Bread and Flowers: Outreach collaboration between the Indianapolis Museum of Art and Flanner House for audience enhancement of the arts
- HIV Program
- Indianapolis Neighborhood Housing Partnership (INHP)
- Legal Service Outreach

The city of Indianapolis has one of the strongest economies in the country. It has broken records for job creation and business investment.

The Program(s)

Project SEED

Indianapolis. A program that is geared toward helping students in the Indianapolis area is called **Project SEED**. Project SEED is a non-profit organization of mathematicians and scientists from industry, universities, and research corporations who socratically teach advanced, conceptually-oriented mathematics to at-risk students. By successfully discovering concepts from algebra, calculus, and other higher mathematics, these student experience significant growth in academic confidence and critical thinking skills.

Project SEED was founded in 1963 by William Johntz. Johntz realized, while teaching remedial mathematics at Berkley High School, that many of his students were burdened with a history of school failure experiences that decreased their academic self-confidence, which in turn resulted in poor performance. Rather than focus on traditional remediation, he decided to provide students with positive learning experiences. Johntz developed an approach that presented a curriculum of advanced mathematics using a highly interactive teaching method and used this successfully with his high school students.

Project SEED has grown to reach hundreds of teachers and thousands of students every year in cities including Dallas, Detroit, the Philadelphia area, and the San Francisco Bay area. Project SEED is supported by school districts, corporations, foundations, and communities which see the need to increase students' academic success, critical thinking skills, and mathematics ability in order to improve students chances of future success.

The tidy metropolis, Indianapolis, on the prairie is a magnet for corporate headquarters and amateur sporting events, and its cultural offerings—including a symphony orchestra and an enormous children museum—are world class.

♦ ♦ ♦
References

Carpenter, A. (1991). *Indiana*. New York: Children's Press

Indiana Project SEED, Indianpolis, Indiana.

Indiana. *World book encyclopedia*. (1998 ed.).

Website

chetabaker@surf-ici.com

CHAPTER 12

The State: Iowa

The state of Iowa is located in the Midwest of the United States. It entered the union on December 28, 1846 as the twenty-ninth state. President Herbert C. Hoover was born in Iowa.

Iowa is also known as the **Hawkeye State**. This name is in honor of Chief Black Hawk, a Sauk Indian. The Sauk Indians occupied Iowa when the white settlers arrived. They welcomed the settlers to share their land.

According to the 1990 census, Iowa had 2,776,755 inhabitants. Whites made up 96.6 percent of the population and blacks, 11.7 percent; additional groups included 7,217 Native Americans, 4,618 people of Korean origin, 4,442 people of Chinese ancestry, 3,374 people of Laotian background, 3,021 Asian Indians, and 2,882 people of Vietnamese descent. Approximately 32,650 residents were of Hispanic ancestry. Roman Catholics formed the largest religious group, followed by the Methodists and Lutherans.

The state of Iowa housed the event which sparked the Civil War. In 1857 the United States Supreme Court ruled that Dred Scott, a freed slave, be returned to his owner. He was brought to Iowa.

The capital is Des Moines. The state bird is the eastern gold finch; the state tree, oak; and the state flower, wild rose.

The Person(s)

Dr. Shannon C'deBraca

Des Moines. Dr. Shannon C'deBaca is one of Des Moines, Iowa's outstanding citizens. Through education, she has used teaching to its greatest potential to touch the lives of young people in America. She has devoted 20 years of her life to clearing paths for the 3,000 students who have passed her way.

One of Dr. C'deBaca's greatest contributions has been one of the many programs she has developed called Kid Chem. This program allows and involves high school students going into elementary classrooms and teaching younger students science concepts. She continues to work through these programs that she has developed to touch and enhance the lives of children.

Dr. C'deBaca is a chemistry teacher at Council Bluff in Des Moines, Iowa. She is a teacher representative on the National Standard Committee, and is responsible for writing the science standards and collecting student data for publication in the performance standards book. In fact, Dr. C'deBaca holds the distinct honor of being the only representative on the committee in the area of science.

Some of her many accomplishments include:

- A $25,000 Milliken Award for Outstanding Teaching and was selected as the Council Bluffs Teacher of the Year
- Runner-up for the Iowa Teacher of the Year. She is active with Iowa Public Television and was honored for her use of audio visuals in the classroom. One of her major awards was National Science Teacher of the Year.

Dr. C'deBaca has further impacted society through her teaching methods and her participation in organizations that promote excellence in education. All of her students are in consensus that she teaches more than what is in the textbooks.

The Program(s)

Iowa Child Abuse Prevention Program

Statewide. The Iowa Child Abuse Prevention Program is a program geared toward helping children. In 1982 the Iowa legislature established this statewide program in response to the need to prevent child abuse. This program was established to create councils to operate in six major areas:

- **Crisis Nursery** has six projects. It served 300 families along with 557 children and 27,100 hours of care. There are 144 volunteers.
- **Home Visitor** has 28 projects. It served 5,514 families along with 2,634 children. There are 463 volunteers who have worked 11,009 hours.
- **Parent Education** has 23 projects. It served 782 families along with 1,335 children. There are 383 volunteers who have worked 5,319 hours.
- **Respite Care** has 19 projects. It served 1,267 families along with 2,194 children. There are 737 volunteers who have worked 7,167 hours.
- **Sexual Abuse Prevention** has 16 projects. It served 22,231 children. Staff hours amounted to 2,890. There are 580 volunteers who have worked 3,456 hours.
- **Young Parents** has 13 projects. It served 389 families along with 456 children. Staff hours amounted to 7,720. There are 600 volunteers who have worked 6,346 hours.

This large organization has created smaller councils to continue to serve in the protection of the children. News is spreading throughout the state about the wonderful work these volunteers and staff members are doing. Expansion is in the plan.

◆ ◆ ◆

References

Carpenter, A. (1979). The new enchantment of America, Iowa. Chicago: Regensteiner Publishing Enterprises, Inc.

Goodman, S. (1999, March). Teaching life's lessons. *The Des Moines Register*, p. 2.

Horton, L., & Hillerich, R. (1991). America the beautiful, Iowa. Chicago: Children's Press.

Prevent Child Abuse Iowa, 550 Eleventh Street, Suite 200, Des Moines, Iowa.

Thompson, K. (1986). Portrait of America, Iowa. Milwaukee: Raintree Publishers, Inc.

CHAPTER 13

The State: Kansas

The state of Kansas is sometimes referred to as Midway, USA. It entered the union January 29, 1861 as the thirty-fourth state. The name of the state is taken from the Kansas River, which was named for the Kansa, a Sioux tribe. Kansas is called the **Sunflower State**.

According to the 1990 census, Kansas had 2,477,574 inhabitants. Whites made up 90.1 percent of the population and blacks, 5.8 percent; additional population groups included 21,767 Native Americans, 6,577 people of Vietnamese background, 5,330 people of Chinese descent, 4,016 people of Korean ancestry, and 3,956 people of Asian Indian origin. Approximately 93,700 people were of Hispanic origin. Roman Catholics, Baptists, and Methodists formed the largest religious groups.

In 1803, Kansas was acquired by the United States as part of the Louisiana Purchase. The geographical location of Kansas has earned it the nickname "Heart of America." Kansas is located in the exact center of the continental United States. The fertile fields of Kansas has also earned it another nickname, "Breadbasket of America." Kansas has been given this nickname because it houses the nation's largest granary.

The capital is Topeka. The state bird is the western meadowlark; the state tree, cottonwood; and the state flower, wild native sunflower.

The Person(s)

Mayor Emanuel Cleaver

Kansas City. Kansas City's Mayor Emanuel Cleaver is not only a politician who represents the voting age population, but he is also a concerned coordinator and spokesman for Kansas City's youth as well. The youth of Kansas City is important to Mayor Cleaver because he believes the fate of our future will one day be dependent upon them. Mayor Cleaver wasn't convinced that the educational system and the working parent were enough to provide for the many demands and needs of Kansas City's youth. He felt that such a task needed to be a community-wide effort in order to be effective. Mayor Cleaver was also concerned with the number of youth involved in violent crimes and drug-related activities. He saw an urgent need for young people to have supervised and guided activities to combat the troubles that often accompany idle mindedness; the first of his solutions was Night Hoops.

Night Hoops was a program designed to offer young people a positive alternative during the summer months. At first, the program consisted of a league in which 16 basketball teams played regulated ball at one location. The ages of the men ranged from 18-25, a targeted age group for crime among males. Also the time in which the games are played is from 10 p.m. to 2 a.m. This time frame was also selected by the Mayor because of the tendency for crimes to be committed during these hours. At the present, The Night Hoops Program has grown to include female teams, volleyball, younger age groups, sports clinic and training, expanded educational workshops, and new locations throughout the city.

Mayor Cleaver's second solution to keep Kansas City's youth out of trouble was his Hot Summer Nights Program. During the morning this program provided a variety of activities for young people such as swimming, dancing, games, and other supervised activities. A lot of the volunteers that help supervise are parents.

Mr. Chris Whittle

Wichita. Mr. Chris Whittle, a Caucasian American, is an outstanding person in Wichita Kansas where he resides. He has dedicated his time to helping multicultural children. One of the contributions that he has made is called The Edison Project (K-12). His initial interest is to create innovative schools that operate at current public schools' spending levels and provide all students with an academically excellent education rooted in democratic values.

The Edison Project establishes partnership schools in contract with a local school district or as part of a character school initiative. In the schools it contracts with, the Edison Project is responsible for implementing the educational program, technology plans, and management systems. It is also accountable to the communities it serves for the performance of the schools. In Edison partnership schools, authority must be decentralized as possible, and each decision-making unit must be accountable for results.

The Edison Project intends to enable high school graduates to perform college-level work. It also strives to foster in every student an appreciation of the arts, a commitment to health and fitness, an understanding of right and wrong, and desire to participate responsibly in a democratic society. The design is composed of ten integral parts: Schools organized for every student's success; better use of time; rich and challenging curriculum; teaching methods that motivate; careful assessment that provides real accountability; a professional environment for teachers; technology for an information age; new partnership with parents; schools tailored to the community; and backed by a system that serves.

Mr. Whittle was founder of Whittle Communications, which from 1970 to 1989 was one of America's largest student publishers. Also in 1989, he converted its print business to electronic ones, launching Channel One, which was the first national electronic news system. Today, it serves as many as 12,000 middle and high schools throughout the U. S., providing 8,000,000 students with domestic and international news.

The Program(s)

The Edison Project

Wichita. The Edison Project, founded in 1991, is the country's leading private manager of public schools. Edison has now implemented its school design in 51 public schools, including many charter schools, which it operates under management contracts with local school districts and charter school boards. Approximately 24,000 students currently attend Edison partnership schools.

Generally, students in Edison schools are representative of the communities in which the schools reside. Edison offers a comprehensive education program designed to work for students of all types from those who find school difficult to those for whom success comes easily. Some facts about Edison are

- As a system, Edison serves a student population that is 45 percent African American, 32 percent Caucasian, 18 percent Hispanic, 2 percent Asian, and 2 percent other.
- Sixty percent of all Edison students are eligible for the federal government's free or reduced price lunch program.
- The majority of Edison schools qualify as school-wide Title I projects.
- The lowest percentage of free and reduced price lunch for children at any Edison school is 27 percent.
- Fifteen percent of all Edison students receive English as a Second Language or Bilingual Education.
- Nine percent of all Edison students receive special education services, a figure close to the percentages of students receiving special education in the respective communities of which Edison schools are a part.

Make-A-Wish Foundation of Kansas

Statewide. The **Make-A-Wish Foundation** is dedicated to granting the single wish of Kansas children between the ages of two-and-a-half to eighteen who have life threatening illnesses or medical conditions. The program in Kansas granted its first wish in January 1985.

Some of the wishes granted include
- Sending a 7-year-old LaCrosse boy to meet Troy Aikman of the Dallas Cowboys
- Building a backyard play set for a 6-year-old Lawrence girl
- Sending a 7-year-old boy from Wichita on a shopping spree to Toys'R'Us
- Providing a TV, VCR, and a selection of tapes to a 6-year-old Emporia girl
- Sending many wish kids from all over Kansas to Disney World

Some corporate donations and external donations made to date include:
- 1998 Scoops Sponsors – Old Town Association, Coleman Factory Outlet and Museum, Rowdy Joe's Steakhouse/Redbeard Saloon, Hero Sports Bar and the River City Brewery
- 1998 Home Town Buffet Car Show
- Hair Force One, Independence
- Java Villa
- Chevy's Finest Classics Car Club
- United Methodist Church Vacation Bible School

This program has become very successful not only in the state of Kansas, but also nationwide. Since the Kansas branch was formed, more than 275 wishes have been granted. The Make-A-Wish Foundation of Kansas estimates a positive direct impact on 152 individuals each year, plus indirect impact on countless volunteers and donors. The program owes its success to the volunteers, businesses, and corporate donations, internal and external fundraisers, grants from public and private foundations, and the efforts of many service clubs and organizations.

Midwestern Prevention Project

Kansas City. **The Midwestern Prevention Project** has been one of the most successful programs in deterring drug and alcohol use among adolescents in Kansas City since the mid 1980s. The program was first thought of after a 1979 report by the United States Surgeon General and other national reports were geared at reducing the use of tobacco, alcohol, and other drugs that have been noted to cause health problems.

The program first started out as a six-year experiment in which 15 communities that make up the Kansas City Metropolitan area implemented mass media programming, school-based educational programs, parent education and organization, community organizations, and various health components to prevent adolescent drug abuse. Since its beginning, the Midwestern Prevention Project has spearheaded other drug preventative groups such as Project CHOICE and the Kauffman Foundation.

The success of the Midwestern Prevention Project showed a significant reduction in the use of tobacco, alcohol, and marijuana. In the program's first year, tobacco use among adolescents fell from 24 percent to 17 percent; alcohol use fell from 16 percent to 11 percent; and the use of marijuana fell from 10 percent to 7 percent. Today, the program's school based educational programs are still being implemented and rendering similar results. Directors of the program believe that their school-based programs are successful because they educate would-be users of the harmful effects of drug use.

Drug abuse in the Unites States, including the abuse of tobacco, alcohol, marijuana, and illicit substances such as cocaine, is implicated in one third to half of lung cancers and coronary heart disease in adults and in the majority of violent deaths (homicides, suicides, and accidents) in youth.

A preventive intervention model that uses multiple environmental influences might be required to effect long-term changes in adolescent drug use. These influences could be used to support and extend prevention skills learned initially in a school program and to promote a consistent community norm for not using drugs.

♦ ♦ ♦
References

Cleaver, E. (1998). Kansas City invest in its youth. *Nation's City's Weekly*, p. 3.

Kansas. *Collier's encyclopedia*. (1991 ed.).

Kansas. *Encyclopedia americana*. (1997 ed.).

Carpenter, A. (1980). The new enchantment of America. Publishing Enterprise.

Kent, Z. (1990). America the beautiful, Kansas. Chicago Press.

Make-A-Wish Foundation of Kansas, 2016 North Amidon, Wichita, Kansas.

Pentz, M., Dwyer, J., MacKinnon, D. Flay, P., Hansen, W., Wang, E., & Johnson,A. (1989). A multicommunity trial for primary prevention of adolescent drug abuse. *JAMA*, pp. 3259-3266.

Topeka. *Collier's encyclopedia*. (1991 ed.)

Thomas, B. (1997). Plessy v. Ferguson: A brief history with documents. Boston: Bedford Books.

CHAPTER 14

The State: Kentucky

The state of Kentucky is one of the East South Central states of the United States. It entered the union on June 1, 1792 as the fifteenth state. The name Kentucky probably came from the Indian word ***Kentake***, popularly translated as "meadowland" or "prairie." The state's nickname is the **Bluegrass State**, for the unusual bluish-green stemmed grass of the Lexington area. The state has been called the "Dark and Bloody Ground" because of the many battles between the white settlers and Indians in early history. Louisville is the largest city.

According to the 1990 census, Kentucky had 3,685,298 inhabitants. Whites constitute 92 percent of the population and blacks, 7.1 percent; additional population groups include 5,614 Native Americans, 2,972 people of Korean origin, 2,922 people of Indian origin, 2,736 people of Chinese origin, 2,513 people of Japanese origin, and 2,193 people of Filipino origin. Approximately 22,000 Kentucky residents are of Hispanic origin. Baptists constitute the largest single religious group followed by Roman Catholics, Methodists, and Disciples of Christ.

Kentucky is a well-known state due to a number of attractions. One, in particular, is the Kentucky Derby.

The capital is Frankfort. The state bird is the cardinal; the state tree, Kentucky coffee; and the state flower, goldenrod.

The Person(s)

Dr. Deborah Grubb

Morehead. Dr. Deborah Grubb is from Morehead, Kentucky. She takes an interest in promoting healthy schools because she believes that "everyday, students and teachers are exposed to environmentally unsafe schools and homes that can influence their overall health and mental capabilities." She further asserts that most of the problem lies in America's school buildings.

Dr. Grubb is a successful author and is chair of the Department of Leadership and Secondary Education at Morehead State University. She has a Doctor of Philosophy degree and is an assistant professor.

In her article entitled "Is Your School Sick? Five Threats to Healthy Schools," she and co-author Thomas Diamantes state some of the most common causes of sick building syndrome in schools:

- Poor design or installation of the ventilation system
- Altered ventilation system, usually to save energy
- Students in crowded schools doing work that was not planned for in the original building design (e.g., using kilns in art classes or metal working in industrial arts classes)
- Poorly or incorrectly maintained ventilation system, usually due to ignorance or efforts to save money

Further, the authors define the term *sick building syndrome* as a host of mysterious illnesses thought to result from tightly sealed, poorly ventilated buildings. They state that the "symptoms, which are often diffuse, non-specific, and flu-like include headache, nausea, congestion, drowsiness, dizziness, and general respiratory distress."

Mayor Jerry Abramson

Louisville. One person who is not only visible but making a difference in the lives of children is Mayor Jerry Abramson. He resides in Louisville. Mayor Abramson launched the initial "Campaign for Kids" in 1997. The recent campaign is a sequel to the initial one.

The Campaign for Kids was launched in response to the President's Summit for America's Future, a national effort to reach two million at-risk youths through volunteerism by the year 2000. The local campaign gave 200 groups an opportunity to donate time, talent, resources, and also prompted a flood of calls to the volunteer connection line.

According to C. Dennis Riggs, president and chief executive officer of the Community Foundation, the flood shows that the hearts of the community are pretty big. He also expressed that the "people not only give generously, but they stand for values and lifting up young people."

Before the Campaign for Kids started last year, Metro United Way's Volunteer Connection line received about 20 calls a week, said United Way President Robert C. Reifsnyder. But the campaign boosted that number to more than 100 calls a week soon after.

Despite such success, Mayor Abramson said the sequel to the campaign is needed because social ills such as drugs, gangs, child abuse, and teen pregnancy persist. He noted that a third of the community's 700,000 youths are considered to be at risk of suffering from the effects of such social problems.

Although the focus is on individuals, the campaign also is accepting calls from organizations that would be willing to make a commitment to help volunteer effort through 2000. Mayor Abramson is urging people to make a difference in the lives of others. He says that the positive momentum is high and that the people have to keep it up.

The Program(s)

Child Watch

Paducah. The Child Watch Program is located in Paducah, Kentucky. It is a non-profit grassroots organization that was established on August 7, 1984. Child Watch was organized to educate the public about the high incidence of child abuse/neglect in McCracken County.

Since 1984, Child Watch has evolved into a multi-faced organization providing programs that are necessary to meet the needs of the children and victims of the McCraken County community. Volunteers are trained to implement the program areas of Child Watch under the supervision of the Child Watch staff. The Child Watch organization is dependent on community support and grants to fund each of the Child Watch programs. It is because of the donations from many segments of society such as corporations, private citizens, churches, and others that all services provided are free to the public.

Parents, church parishioners, corporations, and other concerned agencies see the need for such programs and are just willingly donating time and money to the cause. The citizens believe that this is a positive way to save the community from the many ills that are seen on television in other places, read about, and even on a large scale witnessed in the small town of Paducah.

Child Watch is very successful. It is the recipient of the following distinguished awards: Attorney General's Certificate of Merit Award; CASA "Outstanding Victim Advocate" Award; The Commonwealth of Kentucky Salute; The Governor's Volunteer Activist Award among others.

Student Technology Leadership

Statewide. The Student Technology Leadership Program involves children, students, adults, and teachers. It works in conjunction with technology-enhanced education for staff development, where student-and-teacher interaction is essential.

Since the children were thought to be the state's most powerful resource, the program, which harnesses student enthusiasm and technical expertise, was launched statewide. Individual schools determined the form these staff development efforts would actually take. Almost 500 schools have implemented their own Student Technology Leadership Program, delivering technology training to students, faculty, and other staff members in resourceful ways.

During the program's first two years, a $1000 start-up grant was available. To obtain funding, teachers and students had to work together to develop an action plan. A wide variety of activities received support.

In an article entitled, "Teach Your Teachers Well: Successful Strategies for Staff Development," Janna Tobbe Hickey of Kentucky's Department of Education states, "We have some schools where students work in tech crews, mentoring teachers who are having problems using newer technology. Teachers schedule the tech crew to come in during a lesson. That way, they can focus on teaching while students take care of the technology."

The article further summarized the benefits of one school district:
- Independent School District #196 in Rosemount, Minnesota received $5 million for technological improvements in 1994
- The Minnesota school system installed a local area network in 30 schools and two district offices, a computer in virtually every classroom, and a wide area network to connect all 32 sites.
- Before this technology infusion, the district computer ratio ranged from one machine for 18 students to one machine for seven students.

♦ ♦ ♦

References

Fradin, D. (1993). From sea to shining sea: Kentucky. Chicago: Children's Press.

Grubb, D., & Diamantes, T. (1998, March/April). Is your school sick: Five threats to healthy schools. *The Clearing House*, 71, (4), pp. 202-206.

Holzberg, C. (1997, March). Teach your teachers well: Successful strategies for staff development. *Technology & Learning*, 17, pp. 34, 36.

Kentucky. *World book encyclopedia.* (1998 ed.).

McNair, S. (1988). America, the beautiful Kentucky. Chicago: Children's Press.

Website

http://www..courier-journal.com

CHAPTER 15

The State: Louisiana

The state of Louisiana is one of the West South Central states of the United States. It entered the union on April 30, 1812 as the eighteenth state. Louisiana is called the **Pelican State.**

According to the 1990 census, Louisiana had 4,219,973 inhabitants. Whites made up 67.3 percent of the population and blacks, 30.8 percent; additional population groups included some 18,361 Native Americans, 17,598 people of Vietnamese extraction, 5,430 people of Chinese descent, 5,083 people of Asian Indian background, and 3,731 people of Filipino origin. Approximately 93,000 people were of Hispanic background.

Louisiana lagnaippe, a little something extra given free by way of good measure, includes the following: Bayou Lafourche is the home of the longest street in the world; Louisiana is the largest producer of oysters in the United States; Avery Island's salt mine is the oldest in the Western Hemisphere; Louisiana has 2,482 islands; The Lake Ponchartrain Causeway is the world's largest bridge built entirely over water; Louisiana's government has operated from five different capital cities throughout its history; The site of the oldest known civilization is Poverty Point in West Carroll Parish.

The capital is Baton Rouge. The state bird is the eastern brown pelican; the state tree, bald cypress; and the state flower, the magnolia.

The Person(s)

Ms. Margaret A. Brown

Shreveport. Ms. Margaret A. Brown was born in 1942 in Shreveport, Louisiana. Reared in a loving African American family, Ms. Brown excelled in the Caddo Parish School System. She received a Bachelor of Science degree in biology from Southern University and A & M College, Baton Rouge, Louisiana, and a Master of Education degree in Secondary School Administration and Supervision from Centenary College in Shreveport.

While completing her education, Ms. Brown served as a mathematics and science teacher and single-parent consultant for Caddo Parish Public Schools. She also served at the School Away from School, an alternative program for pregnant high school students.

Her professional activities include TAPSIS: Teenaged Parents Stay in School, a dropout prevention program. She organized, arranged, and appeared in a five-part series on dropout prevention strategies that aired on KTBS TV in Shreveport.

TAPSIS provides services for all races and backgrounds but is comprised of teens of lower socio-economic standards. This program is geared toward helping all teenaged parents to become economically self-sufficient, attain parenting skills necessary to raise well rounded children, and attain the knowledge required to be functional adults. TAPSIS has graduated many mothers and fathers since 1992 and continues to provide services to the teen parents of the Shreveport area.

Ms. Brown's professional involvement with TAPSIS and other programs gained her recognition as Caddo Parish's Teacher of the Year (1986), Educator of the Year-- Senior High Division (1981), and Principal of the Year (1995).

Ms. Brown continues to serve as the Caddo Parish Public School System principal for the Alternative School Program at the Oak Terrace/J. B. Harville Alternative School.

Mr. Darryl Kilbert

New Orleans. One of New Orleans' most troubled schools is undergoing serious changes. Mr. Darryl Kilbert, principal at Alcee Fortier High School is reigning as the Joe Clark of the 1990s. (Joe Clark is a principal who practices "tough love." A movie was based on his character). As the new principal of the school, Mr. Kilbert isn't wasting time launching his no-nonsense approach to stabilize Fortier and get rid of its bad "apples."

During the 1996-97 academic term, the New Orleans public schools with public attention, focused on Mr. Kilbert, 39, a Dillard University graduate and 21-year veteran educator on a mission to raise test scores, improve discipline at one of the city's most troubled schools, and to erase the scars left by a playground brawl last April that led to the arrests of 27 students.

Unlike Joe Clark, Mr. Kilbert is not relying on the bull horn and baseball bat. The community supports Mr. Kilbert's bold reforms. He sent home letters to over 300 Fortier students urging them to shape up their academic and behavior records or go elsewhere. He wants the students of Alcee Fortier High School to have a positive sense of direction.

The school has been setting up conferences with parents whose children are on the critical list. These students have numerous tardies, absences, and report cards filled with Fs. Mr. Kilbert wants a greater accountability and involvement from parents.

Before arriving at Fortier, Mr. Kilbert was principal at Myrtle Banks Elementary School. He was offered a position at the high school and he didn't hesitate to take the job. He wanted the school to re-establish its good reputation. In the past decades, the school has been perceived by many as a dumping ground for troubled students. Some parents had doubts about entrusting their children at Fortier until they heard about Darryl Kilbert and his new no-nonsense approach for academic success and discipline.

Now, the parents and community are rallying behind Mr. Kilbert 100 percent. The students are motivated to want to succeed and change the school's reputation.

The Program(s)

Building Blocks

New Orleans. A new method of scheduling is getting high marks across the New Orleans area and nationwide. **Building Blocks**, formerly known as block scheduling is a new approach to learning that lets students concentrate on four courses each semester instead of seven year-long courses.

Building Blocks is designed for all students in high school. The program is designed to improve school performance. The advantages of Building Blocks are (1) the promotion of personalized instruction and (2) giving teachers more time for varied instructional styles. Sixty schools have joined in the program statewide.

In the New Orleans area, the program began about three years ago. It was then known as four-by-four scheduling. The first schools to try block scheduling were Destrehan High School in St. Charles Parish, Riverdale High in Jefferson Parish and De La Salle Catholic High in New Orleans.

The concept of block scheduling was implemented after administration from De La Salle studied an alternate program pioneered at schools in Philadelphia, Denver, and Atlanta. A survey done by the Orleans Parish School Board showed the students and faculty liked the new approach. The schools participating in Building Blocks have shown an increase in grade point averages.

Although there are some drawbacks (A survey done by the College Board showed that students who completed advanced placement courses under block scheduling scored poorly on exams), many high schools throughout New Orleans have reported gains in student and teacher attendance and the number of students on the honor roll as a result of block scheduling.

TAPSIS

Shreveport. TAPSIS (Teenaged Parents Stay in School) has as its mission statement a community of educators, other caring citizens, and organizations, dedicated to the teaching, learning, and supportive services for the success of all teen parents and their children.

TAPSIS' emphases and strategies include:

- **Economic self-sufficiency and lifelong learning.** TAPSIS professionals engage every teen parent in developing a career plan and pursuing a planned program of study to prepare her for employment and further education. They seek work-based learning experiences for teen parents.
- **Removal of barriers to school completion.** TAPSIS professionals coach every teen parent in learning about and using cost-effective supportive services to continue in school: Afforable day care, dependable transportation, academic tutoring, sources of learning materials, supplies, and other support.
- **Investment in parenting skills and behaviors.** TAPSIS professionals and volunteers teach teen parents to care for themselves and their children: Prenatal care; parenting education courses and summer parenting camp; nutrition; wholesome, low-cost family recreation; discipline; and joy in learning.

The components of the TAPSIS Program consists of career planning, prenatal exercise, parenting and childcare, development of life/social skills, peer advocacy programs, support groups, self-esteem activities, grandparents workshops, vocational testing and guidance, childcare assistance, and a design team (advisory group).

The program is the brainchild of Margaret A. Brown, a Shreveport educator and now principal at J. B. Harville Alternative School. Ms. Brown witnessed the progressive dropping out of young mothers once the baby was delivered when she first began at the Alternative School. This inspired her to make a difference.

◆ ◆ ◆

References

Brown, M. (1998). *TAPSIS Handbook.* Shreveport, Louisiana.

Louisiana. *World book encyclopedia.* (1994 ed.).

Nabonne, R. (1997, May). Fortier principal cleans house, raises standards. *New Orleans Schools' Newsletter*, p. A-14.

Nabonne, R. (1998, January). Building blocks. *New Orleans Schools' Newsletter*, p. B-1.

CHAPTER 16

The State: Massachusetts

The state of Massachusetts is one of the New England states of the United States. It entered the union on February 6, 1788 as the sixth of the original 13 states. When still a colony, it had become an important intellectual center, known for Harvard University and the cultural institutions of Boston. Massachusetts is called the **Bay State** after the Massachusetts Bay, the site of the Puritans' colony.

According to the 1990 census, Massachusetts had 6,016,425 inhabitants. Whites made up 89.8 percent of the population and blacks, 5 percent; additional groups included 53,792 people of Chinese origin, 19,719 people of Indian origin, 15,449 people of Vietnamese origin, 14,050 people of Cambodian origin, 11,857 Native Americans, and 11,744 people of Korean origin. More than 287,000 Massachusetts residents are of Hispanic origin. Roman Catholics constitute the largest single religious group, followed by Baptists, Jews, Episcopalians, and Methodists.

Massachusetts is famous for its summer resorts, such as the sand beaches of Cape Cod. Presidents John Adams, John Quincy Adams, John F. Kennedy, and George Bush were born in the state and President Calvin Coolidge spent most of his life in Massachusetts.

The capital is Boston. The state bird is the chickadee; the state tree, American elm; and the state flower, the mayflower.

The Person(s)

Dr. Marie McCormick

Cambridge. Dr. Marie McCormick is on the staff for the Harvard Center for Children's Health Mission. She attended John Hopkins Medical School in 1971 and the John Hopkins School of Hygiene and Public Health. She chairs the Department of Maternal and Child Health.

The Harvard Center for Children's Health was created in 1995 to translate what they "know" about children's health into what they "do" to improve children's health and well-being. The faculty and staff conduct research to improve their understanding of what places children at risk for health and development and which programs and services are effective in preventing these risks.

Dr. McCormick's research involves epidemiologic and health services research investigations in the areas related to infant mortality and the outcomes of high-risk neonates. Her current projects involve the outcomes of infants' experiences, neonatal complications like low birth weight, and interventions potentially ameliorating adverse outcomes.

Another project deals with the evaluation of programs designed to improve the health of families and children. One of her specific studies is the Infant Health and Development Program. This program obtains early school-age data on a multi-site cohort of low birth weight pre-term children who participate in a randomized trial of an early childhood education intervention program.

She is also working with the Maternal and Child Community Health Consortium with the Boston Neighborhood Health Centers for focus on women's health and health care use following pregnancy.

Her publications' abstracts are available through the National Library of Science Public Medical Services.

Dr. Mitchell Resnick

Cambridge. Dr. Mitchell Resnick is doing something outstanding to help the children of the multicultural society. Dr. Resnick is making toys for children of the digital age. He has also established a non-profit organization, a center for children learning technology.

Dr. Resnick was born and raised in Philadelphia where he always enjoyed toys. His mother always tried to encourage him to study more science and technology, instead of playing with toys all of the time. Dr. Resnick decided to add both a favorite hobby for kids and a learning subject and environment. This is how he incorporated science, technology, and toys together.

Dr. Resnick has computerized Lego blocks, intelligent beads, and kits that allow children to fashion their own scientific instruments. These toys enable students to learn more about technology and science. The colors of the blocks attract students with different computerized chips. These computerized chips enable students to build certain items that the students want to build. He gives out computerized blocks to students who are unable to afford the computerized blocks. The students have to write a letter explaining why they want computerized blocks. Dr. Resnick gives more than fifty Lego blocks a day. He says he has not invented this learning toy for a profit, but instead for a learning experience. He has established a learning center that enables children to learn how to work on computers and even shows them how to build them. He uses his computerized Lego blocks in the process of learning.

Dr. Resnick is part of the laboratory's view "Toys of Tomorrow" project, a partnership with Hasboro, Mattel, Walt Disney, and Lego to design more and better computerized toys. These toys will consist of different toys such as Barbie and other toys children love.

Dr. Resnick is an outstanding individual who is giving back to the community and he is having fun in the process!

The Program(s)

Cops and Kids

Newton. The Bigelow Middle School in Newton, Massachusetts is getting noticed by many top officials. Some of those officials are Newton's police officers. In the city of Newton where education is top priority, a program has been established to make the city and the students better.

Newton, a city in Massachusetts, is known for its low violence rate. It is a city that is not a main attraction in Massachusetts, but where everyone feels like family. Citizens and police officers wanted to keep the city that way. So they decided to develop a program called **Cops and Kids**. The police officer task team of Newton came up with the program.

The Newton Cops and Kids Program is a police grant aimed at providing structured after-school activities to middle school students. The program is made up of the Newton police force, teachers, and the students. The students are male and female, black and white, and include grades 6-8. There is also a small group between the ages of 3-6.

The program is designed to provide positive role models and structured activities. It gives students some organized after-school activities. These after-school activities offer students something concrete to do. The program is also designed to keep the students from getting into trouble. Last year's activities included rock climbing, bowling, canoeing, visiting the capital, and going to the Omni theatre.

The program is offered each Tuesday and Thursday from the time of school dismissal until 6 p.m. There is a small homework component once a week for one hour. The police staff are youth officers with years of experience working with young people.

Hugh O'Brian Youth Leadership Foundation

Boston. In 1958, Hugh O'Brian, a TV actor (Wyatt Earp), returned from Africa inspired by his visit with Dr. Albert Schweitzer. Motivated by the doctor's remarks, "the most important thing in education is to teach young people to think for themselves," Hugh O'Brian established the **Hugh O'Brian Youth Leadership Foundation.** The organization conducts seminars in Canada, the Bahamas, Mexico, and Jamaica.

The mission of the Massachusetts Hugh O'Brian Youth Leadership Foundation is to seek out, recognize, and develop leadership potential in youth. By performing this mission, they inspire and empower leaders of all ages to build a better future. They develop the skills and confidence leaders need through high quality, innovative leadership seminars, Community Leadership Educational Workshops (CLEW), the Alumni Association, and the Board of Directors. They aspire to be the best program in the world; to be widely recognized and respected as a youth organization; to be completely self-funded; and to develop leadership activities beyond traditional programs.

The organization hosts many community service projects. Each September, the National Association of Secondary Public School Principals sends nomination material to all public and private high schools in the United States. Each school selects an outstanding sophomore, based on his/her leadership potential and nominates that student to represent his/her school at the State seminar held each spring. Massachusetts conducts two seminars each year—one in eastern Massachusetts and one in western Massachusetts. All discussions and presentations center on the theme "America's Incentive System," the system which motivates productive activity in our society. The program's "ambassadors" will participate in thought-provoking activities that will enhance their experiences. The emphasis will be on motivating the young people to make a positive contribution to their school and community and to be aware, active, and responsible citizens. Most of the cost is paid by concerned citizens, civic organizations, corporations, and foundations.

♦ ♦ ♦

References

Famighetti, R. (Ed.). (1977). *The world almanac and book of facts.* New Jersey: St. Martin.

Massachusetts. *World book encyclopedia.* (1998 ed.).

McCormick, M., Richardson, D. (1995). Access to neonatal intensive care. *The Future of Children,* 5(1), pp. 162-175.

McCormick, M. (1997). The outcomes of very low birth weight infants: Are we asking the right questions? *Pediatrics,* 99, pp. 869-876.

Wheeling the student. (1999, March). *The Chronicle of Higher Education,* pp. 25,26.

Website

http://bigelowmiddleschool.com

CHAPTER 17

The State: Michigan

The state of Michigan is one of the East North Central states of the United States. It entered the union on January 26, 1837 as the twenty-sixth state. Michigan is called the **Wolverine State** because of the importance of wolverine pelts to early trading posts in the region. Michigan is also known as the "automobile capital of the world."

According to the 1990 census, Michigan had 9,295,297 inhabitants. Whites made up 83.4 percent of the population and blacks, 13.9 percent; additional population groups included 55,131 Native Americans, 23,845 people of Indian origin, 19,145 people of Chinese origin, 16,316 people of Korean origin, 13,786 people of Filipino origin, 10,681 people of Japanese origin, and 6,117 people of Vietnamese origin. Roman Catholics make up the largest religious group, followed by Baptists and Lutherans.

Other interesting facts about Michigan are that Detroit used to be the capital from 1837 to 1847, and Battle Creek, Michigan is the home of Kellogg cereal. Michigan is breath taking at first glance. All eyes are captivated at the beautiful fields. It stands alone in being the only state surrounded by so many Great Lakes. The state is also known for its exquisite mountains and forests.

The capital is Lansing. The state bird is the robin; the state tree, white pine; and the state flower, the apple blossom.

The Person(s)

Sergeant Mark Bos

Lansing. Awarded the MADD Lifesaver Achievement Award for his outstanding contributions in public service is Sergeant Mark Bos. He, along with other law officers, was awarded special awards from MADD (Mothers Against Drunk Driving), which is an organization of people who protest against persons who endanger the lives of others by driving drunk. Sergeant Bos' award was different than the awards given to the other officers because he has displayed tremendous dedication to the cause. He has helped to decrease the number of drunk drivers by making several arrests that helped to take them off the streets and discourage others from driving while intoxicated.

Sergeant Bos makes the time to speak to youth in public schools and has made an exceptional number of drunk driving arrests. He cautions the youth in the schools of the consequences of driving under the influence of alcohol and reminds them of the lifelong damage to the victims' families.

He is a member of the Holland Police Department. He is contributing greatly to the safety and welfare of the people in his community by the daily activities and duties he performs as a public official. Because of the many deaths and accidents caused by drunk driving in Michigan in 1997, Sergent Bos' achievements are especially commendable.

Mr. Ronald E. Hall

Detroit. In the state of Michigan is a well-known man who is recognized for his extended work hours by the name of Ronald E. Hall. Mr. Hall is an African American male. He is 52 years old. He is presently the president and CEO of Michigan Minority Development Council. Mr. Hall has contributed to the city of Detroit by volunteering his time to organizations that serve the interest of Metro Detroit youths.

Some of his involvements with youth organizations include engineering the celebration of Junior Achievement Day in Detroit's public schools; receiving permission for city employees to become Junior Achievement volunteers (Detroit made history by becoming the first city in the nation for this type of volunteerism); working closely with the University of Michigan's College of Engineering to form an alliance for entrepreneurship among underrepresented minority engineering students; former chairman for the Amateur Athletic Union (AAU) Michigan Chapter, which allows for athletic competition in basketball and other sports for young people. Mr. Hall was a part of the effort to propel Child Care Coordinating Council (4Cs) past its $1 million mark.

Being the humble man that he is, Mr. Hall's motivation to help the youth comes from his children and the other part is his love for the city of Detroit. He states that his greatest joy in doing volunteer work is "helping the young people grow up and not get involved with drugs, gangs, and crimes. We're standing on the shoulders of a lot of people who went before us. And all of us are obligated to do what we can so that one day when we meet our forefathers, we can tell them what we did with our freedom."

Fannie Dell Peeples

Detroit. Ms. Fannie Dell Peeples is the true meaning of inspiration, dedication, love, and sincerity. "Peep," as she is called starts her day at 7:30 a.m., and ends at 4:00 p.m. Since 1983, she has volunteered 4,244 hours at Brush Street and Mack Avenue in Detroit at the Children's Hospital of Michigan.

She has also volunteered at the Detroit Receiving Hospital as the chaplain, helped send out death notices to those who have no relatives or friends, and in her apartment helps people pay their bills or shopping. Peep has received numerous awards, some of which include a framed letter from George Bush, the Kiwanis Club Award, and numerous stories about her in newspapers and magazines. Her love for helping people stems from her childhood. She became an orphan at a very early age.

The Program(s)

The Economic Club of Detroit Scholarships

Detroit. A scholarship program of the community foundation for Southeastern Michigan, the **Economic Club of Detroit Scholarship Program** is designed to assists students from the counties of Detroit, Macomb, Oakland, and Wayne to pursue a program of undergraduate education. The program awards two renewable scholarships of $2000 each to students entering college as freshmen.

The Economic Club of Detroit Education Endowment Fund was established to provide educational scholarships to selected individuals residing in the metropolitan Detroit area to attend post-secondary institutions. The Fund is being created with contributions from the Economic Club of Detroit.

The criteria for the program are:
- Strong scholastic performance while in high school or significant academic improvement in each successive year, achieving the equivalency of a 3.2 average in the last two years or at graduation.
- Exemplary leadership and character as demonstrated by extracurricular activities, service in the school and the community, volunteer involvement and paid work experience. Special consideration will be given to those students who have overcome specific hardship in order to achieve their personal and educational goals.
- Academic honors received, class rank, and standardized test scores.
- A written personal statement that describes the applicant's educational plans and career goals, and motivating factors and important experiences which have helped to shape personal philosophy and future goals.
- Family economic need as determined by the Student Aid Report resulting from the free application for federal student aid.

Royal Readathon

Detroit. **Royal Readathon** was developed out of the need for motivating children to read. It is important for children to set aside time, at least 15 minutes or more, for reading. Children are also encouraged when they see parents and others read. The Royal Oak community of Detroit wanted to use the library as a tool to get children interested in reading.

Starting in the summer of 1991, Kathleen A. Balkema, director of the Youth Services challenged parents and children to a readathon as part of the Summer Reading Program. The readathon was going to last eight days for 192 hours non-stop. Parents and children, ages 3 to 13 were to sign up for a thirty-minute reading time slot. The readathon involved the entire community.

Letters, flyers, newspaper articles, and even advertisements on the radio alerted the community of the Royal Readathon. A huge wheel was created to mark each thirty-minute interval. Parents and children used this time to bond and enjoy each other's company. Those children who read at night came in their pajamas. Others were overwhelmed by being at the library at night. One father was able to accomplish a goal of his, which was screaming in the library. Another father found great joy in reading with his three daughters.

The television station was on location at the library and businesses donated a pizza party for the children who participated. Children also received a ribbon for participating, along with parents receiving a certificate. To help encourage the children even more, all of the principals were notified of the children who represented their schools.

Participants received red ribbons with the letters "Royal Reader" imprinted on them. Needless to say, parents and children found this program to be most rewarding and memorable. It motivated the participants to continue lifelong reading habits.

♦ ♦ ♦

References

Balkema, K. (1991, July). Red ribbons for royal readers. *School Library Journal*, (37), p. 30.

Butty, D. (1997, February). Development chief busy making better future for youths. *Detroit News*, p. E1.

Harrington, W., & Thode, S. (1991). So this is what a saint looks like. *Life*, (14), pp. 52-61.

Hintz, M. (1998). Michigan. Michigan: Children's Press.

Michigan. *World book encyclopedia*. (1998 ed.).

Muret, D. (1996, December). Lansing's new oldsmobile park more than just a baseball stadium. *Amusement Business*, pp. 51, 58.

Website

http://www.lineofduty.com/blotter/messages/3689.html

CHAPTER 18

The State: Mississippi

The state of Mississippi is one of the East South Central states of the United States. It entered the union on December 10, 1817 as the twentieth state. Jackson is the largest city. Mississippi is called the **Magnolia State**.

According to the 1990 census, Mississippi had 2,573,216 inhabitants. Whites made up 63.5 percent of the population and blacks, 35.6 percent (a higher proportion than any other state); additional population groups included 8,435 Native Americans, 3,815 people of Vietnamese origin, 2,518 people of Chinese origin, and 1,872 people of Indian origin. About 15,900 Mississippians claim Hispanic ancestry. Baptists form by far the largest religious group, followed by Methodists, Roman Catholics, and Pentecostals.

Some important facts about Mississippi include: Coca-Cola was first bottled in Vicksburg in 1894. Root Beer was invented in Biloxi by Edward Adolf Barq, Sr., in 1898. The nation's first black newspaper was founded by a Mississippian, W. A. Scott. The world's largest shrimp is on display at the Old Spanish Fort Museum in Pascagoula. The world's longest man-made beach is along the Mississippi Gulf Coast. Mississippi has more churches per capita than any other state in the country.

The capital is Jackson. The state bird is the mocking bird; the state tree, magnolia; and the state flower, the magnolia.

The Person(s)

Miss Oseola McCarty

Hattiesburg. Short in statue, but big in heart is how Miss Oseola McCarty can be described. Miss McCarty washed clothes for nearly all of her 87 years of life. All the while, the tiny woman kept a secret that has recently rocked the town's 45,000 residents.

For 60 years, only the local bankers knew that while Miss McCarty was elbow deep in dirty water, she was knee deep in money, having squirreled away what would eventually total nearly a quarter of a million dollars. The town and the world found out about the virtues of washing clothes recently when she decided to give $150,000 to the nearby University of Southern Mississippi, a school she had never visited. The money establishes an endowed scholarship fund, with priority given to needy Black students.

Miss McCarty's work day was always the same: At the first sign of daybreak, she would begin boiling white clothes in a big iron pot, grinding dirty socks and underwear on her old Maid Rite scrub board in water she had drawn from a nearby fire hydrant. She would then wring the clothes and hang them to dry on about 100 feet of line. By the time she reached the end of the line, the clothes at the beginning would be dry. The day ended with her ironing as the sun set.

In the '60s, she bought an automatic washer and dryer, but gave both away after using them once and finding them miserably insufficient. "The washing machine didn't rinse enough and the dryer turned the whites yellow," she said.

The quiet woman never took sick, never complained much and never raised her voice above a whisper. In fact, Miss McCarty's life has been filled with nevers. She never owned a car (she still pushes a buggy about a mile to the local Big Star grocery store), never used her air conditioner (unless visitors insisted).

Miss McCarty retired last December and continues not to want anything, except maybe some new hands.

The Program(s)

Mississippi School for Mathematics and Science Outreach

Statewide. The Mississippi School for Mathematics and Science is committed to pursuing an aggressive program of outreach to benefit the students, teachers, and all citizens of the state of Mississippi. The outreach includes instructional workshops for teachers and programs for students during the school year and in the summer. In keeping with the increasing availability of technology in the classroom, many of the topics are related to technology utilization. Outreach activities include:

- **School-Year Programs for Students.** The Mississippi School for Mathematics and Science faculty has developed a program with West Clay High School called Science Stars. Science Stars is designed to increase student interest in mathematics and science through hands-on activities, mentoring, and seminars. The program meets twice a month on the second and fourth Friday nights from 6:30 until 9:30. Approximately 50 students participated in Science Stars last year.

- **School-Year Instructional Workshops.** The Mississippi School for Mathematics and Science faculty and staff led 15 instructional workshops during the 1996-97 school year. The topics covered by the workshops focused primarily on using technology in the classroom. Three hundred and eight teachers from across the state attended these workshops.

- **Distance Learning.** During the school year, The Mississippi School for Mathematics and Science faculty taught three courses from the MUW studio over ETV's FiberNet System. The courses taught were German I, Probability and Statistics, and Creative Writing. Fifty-six students at four sites were enrolled in the courses.

Other activities included an African American Historic Sites Tour in Columbus and a Cultural/Historical Tour of North Mississippi and Columbus.

♦ ♦ ♦

References

Chapell, K. (1995, December). The washer woman philanthropist: Mississippi senior citizen gives $150,000 to local university. *Ebony*, 51 (2), p. 84.

The 25 most intriguing people of the year. (1995, December). *People*, 44 (26), p. 154.

Website

http://www.msms.doe.k12.ms.us/outreach/1996-97/update.html

CHAPTER 19

The State: Missouri

The state of Missouri is one of the West North Central states of the United States. It entered the union on August 10, 1821 as the twenty-fourth state. Kansas City is the largest city. Missouri is called the **Show Me State**.

According to the 1990 census, Missouri had 5,117,073 inhabitants. Whites made up 87.7 percent of the population and blacks, 10.7 percent; additional population groups included 19,508 Native Americans, 4,380 people of Vietnamese origin, 8,614 people of Chinese origin, 5,624 people of Filipino origin, 5,731 people of Korean origin, and 6,111 people of Indian origin. About 61,700 people are of Hispanic background. Baptists form the largest religious group, followed by Roman Catholics, Methodists, and Lutherans.

The famous Dred Scott case was started in Missouri. In 1846, Scott went to the courthouse in St. Louis. He sued for his freedom. He had lived in places that outlawed slavery. In 1857, the United States Supreme Court ruled that he was still a slave. It also said the Missouri Compromise went against the United States Constitution. The Dred Scott Decision angered antislavery northerners. It helped bring on the Civil War. On January 11, 1865, Missouri outlawed slavery. It was the first slave state to do so.

The capital is Jefferson City. The state bird is the bluebird; the state tree, flowering dogwood, and the state flower, hawthorn.

The Person(s)

Mrs. Laurie Sybert

Lake Ozark. Mrs. Laurie Sybert, a second-grade teacher at Mills Elementary School in the School of the Osage R-II School District, Lake Ozark, has been selected as Missouri's Teacher of the Year for 1998-99.

Mrs. Sybert, who has taught for 12 years, began her career as an elementary music instructor. She has taught elementary classes at the School of the Osage for the past 10 years, and second grade since 1991.

A strong believer in parental involvement, Mrs. Sybert has organized "Family Science Nights" for the past two years, providing an enjoyable way for students to bring their parents and siblings to school and involve them in educational activities. These events are an effective way for school personnel to get better acquainted with parents and to involve them in their children's learning.

While she teaches all subjects, Mrs. Sybert says "science is my absolute love," and science provides the themes for many of her lessons and classroom activities. Her students get involved in many hands-on science activities and practice writing by recording their observations of plants, animals, and seasons. They apply their developing math skills with problems such as calculating how many cups, quarts and gallons of water are needed to fill an aquarium in the classroom.

Mrs. Sybert says her "zeal for learning" is her greatest asset. "I am always eager to hear about any idea that other educators have tried and found to be successful. I never stop at the expected, but try to push myself and my students to want to know and do more," she said in describing her philosophy of teaching.

She is currently working on her master's degree in curriculum and leadership. She chairs her school's science committee, supervises student teachers, and serves as a mentor.

The Program(s)

A Hard Line for Learning

Columbia. A Hard Line for Learning is a program for behaviorally disordered students that combines strict controls with special incentives. The timeout rooms and Safety First position are based on a program developed by Charlie Green, an independent special education consultant in Columbia, who works with school districts and other agencies. The program was fully implemented last year.

Oakland saw a need for the program because school officials wanted an alternative to suspension. They felt students were missing too much class time while on suspension and that some were deliberately getting kicked out of school because they didn't want to be there.

All of the students in the class have been labeled by the school district as "behaviorally disordered," which means that a student's behavior interferes with his learning. Behaviorally disordered is a special education category that can include anything from Attention Deficit and Hyperactivity Disorder to schizophrenia.

The Department of Elementary and Secondary Education has no policy on timeouts or takedowns, leaving those decisions to the individual school districts.

The student is placed in a relatively small area where there are very few distractions, allowing them to focus on themselves, obtain control and be ready to come out. It is important for timeout rooms to have adequate ventilation and a window so teachers can see the students. Also, there should be no objects in the rooms, so students can't injure themselves.

Tim Lewis, associate professor of special education at Missouri University who has done considerable research, says that research shows that timeouts lose their effectiveness if they are used repeatedly.

♦ ♦ ♦

References

Missouri. *World book encyclopedia.* (1996 ed.).

Website

http://www.dese.state.mo.us/news/1998toy.htm

CHAPTER 20

The State: Montana

The state of Montana is one of the Mountain states of the United States. It entered the union on November 8, 1889 as the forty-first state. Billings is the largest city. The rich mineral resources of the western mountain region have earned its nickname the **Treasure State**. The state is also called "Big Sky Country" and the "Last Best Place."

The name Montana is derived from the Spanish word *montana* meaning mountain.

According to the 1990 census, Montana had 799,095 inhabitants. Whites made up 92.7 percent of the population and blacks, 0.3 percent; additional population groups included 47,524 Native Americans, 4,259 people of Asian or Pacific Island; 12,000 people of Hispanic background. Roman Catholics form the largest religious group, followed by Lutherans and Methodists.

Topographically, the state may be divided into two distinct regions: East and west. The eastern portion is part of the Great Plains. It is composed of rolling hills interspersed with low mountains, deep gorges and unusual rock formation. In the north, the fertile soil produces an abundance of high-quality wheat. The grazing land in the south is ideal for raising cattle

The capital is Helena. The state bird is the western meadowlark; the state tree, ponderosa pine; and the state flower, the bitterroot.

The Person(s)

Mr. Chuck Hunter

Helena. Mr. Chuck Hunter is the administrator of Child and Family Services Division. He has worked for this department since October, 1998. He is responsible for the day-to-day operations of the division staff who administer a variety of programs and services that help to protect vulnerable children, youth, and adults, who suffer from abuse or neglect. Services include child protection, foster care, adoption, family preservation and support, and domestic violence prevention. The division works closely with communities and providers to assist families in increasing their ability to nurture and provide for their children.

Prior to his current position, Mr. Hunter was administrator of the Employment Relations Division of Montana's Department of Labor and Industry. His responsibilities included administration of the regulatory function for workers' compensation, the state safety program, the wage and hour program, the state human rights program, and the collective bargaining program for public sector employers. Before assuming that position in 1991, he spent five years managing Montana's unemployment insurance program. His past experiences also include working as an analyst with the Department of Administration, managing a treatment facility in a residential home for delinquent youth, and teaching a variety of classes and group skills to students at the National Technical Institute for the Deaf.

Mr. Hunter's dedication to his work is evident with his educational degrees: He has a Bachelor's Degree in liberal arts from Elmira College and a Master's Degree in experimental education from the University of Colorado. Mr. Hunter decided to farther his education by maintaining a degree in experimental education. This alone proved that he was dedicated in assisting children and adults within a multicultural society.

The Program(s)

Curriculum Innovation: Middle School Approach

Belgrade. No society is immune from the effects of technological change. What happens in one sector can dramatically affect what happens in another area. The need to understand technology and its impact has never been so important as it is today.

Entrepreneurs, with the aid of technological innovation, can live in one state while running their businesses in another. Learning opportunities leading to a better understanding of technological developments are crucial to national economic progress.

Technology education, like other educational disciplines, has recognized the necessity for change. One example is Belgrade Middle School in Belgrade, Montana, a rural school that wanted to make technology education courses available to its students. Recently the Belgrade School Board of Trustees, the school administration and its teachers worked with the Montana State University Department of Agricultural and Technology Education.

All parties involved were well briefed on the plan beforehand. Undergraduate students in technology education conducted "technology learning activities" and presented design briefs to middle school students.

Both course content and grade levels were specific considerations when planners met to write the new curriculum. Approximately 150 students in grades 5-8 would be using the technology education facility daily.

Class schedules were designed that fifth- and sixth-grade students were in the lab for one class period two days each week. Technology education replaced the industrial arts component of the exploratory block for seventh and eighth graders.

The Belgrade Middle School project is a model for Montana professionals seeking to develop technology education programs in middle schools.

♦ ♦ ♦

References

Davis, S. (1992). Curriculum innovation: Middle school approach. *The Vocational Education Journal*, 67, pp. 72-73.

Heinrichs, A. (1991). *America the beautiful*. Montana: Children's Press.

Montana. *Collier's encyclopedia*. (1993 ed.).

Website

Chuhunter@state.mt.us

CHAPTER 21

The State: Nebraska

The state of Nebraska is one of the West North Central states of the United States. It entered the union on March 1, 1867 as the thirty-seventh state. Omaha is the largest city. Nebraska is called the **Cornhusker State**.

According to the 1990 census, Nebraska had 1,578,385 inhabitants. Whites made up 93.8 percent of the population and blacks, 3.6 percent; additional population groups included 12,344 Native Americans, 1,943 people of Korean origin, 1,806 people of Vietnamese origin, and 1,175 people of Chinese origin. Nearly 37,000 Nebraska residents reported Hispanic ancestry. Roman Catholics form the largest religious group, followed by Lutherans and Methodists.

Nebraska produces meats, breakfast cereals, bakery products, telephone equipment, farm machinery, scientific and medical instruments, and medicines. The mining products are oil, clays, sand and gravel, crushed stone, and limestone.

"Equality Before the Law" is the state motto. The state flag was adopted in 1925, and the state seal was adopted in 1867. The name of the state came from the Indian word *nebrathka*, which means "flat water." The white-tailed deer is the state mammal. Some major cities include: Omaha, Lincoln, Grand Island, Bellevue, Kearney, Fremont, Hastings, North Plate, Norfolk, and Columbus.

The capital is Lincoln. The state bird is the western meadowlark; the state tree, western cottonwood; and the state flower, the goldenrod.

The Person(s)

Dr. Wolf Wolfensberger

Lincoln. Dr. Wolf Wolfensberger, of the Nebraska Psychiatric Institute, formulated the Citizen Advocacy in 1966. He is helping people all over the country, especially in Lincoln, Nebraska, where the first Citizen Advocacy was opened in 1970.

The Citizen Advocacy gives help to people who realize the need for and importance of companionship to individuals who are disabled. The Citizen Advocacy works with individuals on a one-to-one basis. By working on a one-to-one basis, an individual that is disabled will become integrated into society, and at the same time, influence society toward a greater understanding of his/her needs and rights.

Dr. Wolfensberger's reason for creating the Citizen Advocacy was to help disabled citizens with emotional support and practical support. During the emotional support, the Citizen Advocacy offers companionship and friendship and encourages protégé involvement in the community through participation in recreational and leisure activities. The Advocate helps develop and extend support network for the protégé so that there isn't a dependence on one person for emotional support.

During the practical support, the Citizen Advocacy encourages independent living by teaching life skills such as budgeting, shopping, and learning to travel alone; thereby, reducing dependency on the Advocate. It also shares experiences with the protégé to introduce and develop problem-solving skills for daily living. Also, the Citizen Advocacy aids the protégé in obtaining medical, social, educational, vocational, financial, and recreational services.

As a result of Dr. Wolf Wolfensberger formulating the first Citizen Advocacy in Lincoln, Nebraska in 1996, a workshop was introduced in March 1971 in Canada to encourage the growth of local committees and the start of progams in major cities.

Mr. Kim N. Lombardi

Omaha. Mr. Kim N. Lombardi is he founder of J.A.Y.D.N., Inc. (Juveniles Against Youth Drinking Now). It was founded in honor of Mr. Lombardi's only son, Jaydn, who was killed in a single car, alcohol related crash.

J.A.Y.D.N., Inc., is a non-profit corporation. It was founded with two goals. First, to get minors off alcohol and second, to get alcohol advertising controlled.

Mr. Lombardi realizes that this battle must be waged at the federal level in order to achieve the goals. For the last three years, he has watched the Nebraska Legislature "do nothing about the problem of underage drinking," he says. He has learned that too many states do very little to control this problem. He has also learned that getting the attention of Washington, D. C., is the path to success. That is his ultimate goal.

Mr. Lombardi travels across the nation, talking to students, teachers, and parents about underage drinking and recruiting their help. An army is being formed to fight the alcohol industry. He was told that when he started this project, one person couldn't make a difference. Now he has hundreds of thousands of "one persons" that are going to make a difference.

Mr. Lombardi, his wife, and two daughters are taking every opportunity to go into the schools, communities, to urge people to get involved. He shares the memories of his son, how vibrant he was, the future he had before him, the dreams—all shattered because of that one accident.

Mr. Lombardi believes that if people see him and hear his story (particularly young people in high school), they will think twice before drinking. Whenever he speaks before a young crowd, he captures their attention about the lost dreams of his son—here today, gone tomorrow.

Mr. Lombardi is urging people to join the fight against underage drinking. It is a battle that must be won. Underage drinking is out of control.

The Program(s)

Youth Services International, Inc. (YSI)

Statewide. Youth Services International, Inc., is in the business of reclaiming young lives. This is done through the development and implementation of programs that meet the needs of various stakeholders, governmental agencies, adjudicated youth, Youth Services International, Inc.'s employees, citizens within communities, and youth advocates.

Youth Services International, Inc.'s programs encompass a holistic approach to education, training, and socialization of youth in order to prepare them to re-enter society as positive, contributing, taxpaying members of their community. Youth Services International, Inc.'s programs are designed to equip youth with the skills, educational base, and behavioral norms to enable the youth to be successful in the workplace, the school, and the community.

The programs are comprised of four major components: Education, vocational training, group living (socialization), and recreation. Applied consistently throughout these components are behavioral management principles that are intended to change dramatically the thinking and behavior of delinquent youth, teach basic life skills, and reinforce the principle that success begins with appropriate, acceptable behavior. Consequently, the program's components interlock and blend together to form a cohesive, consistent program designed to develop a youth that is fully equipped to meet the challenges of life in a responsible, acceptable manner. In addition, Youth Services International, Inc.'s principal priority is to provide programs in a safe and secure environment for the community.

The goal of the Youth Services International, Inc., is to provide, through the application of its components, for the transition of the youth back into the community.

People's City Mission

Lincoln. The People's City Mission Program is located in Lincoln, Nebraska. The purpose for the People's City Mission is to help establish among the impoverished, productive and life-changing relations with Jesus Christ by proclaiming the salvation message through compassionate rescue ministries. It is an effective outreach that serves as a channel between the Christian community and those who are less fortunate. It has been a vital part of Lincoln since its door opened in 1907.

There is no pre-condition for receiving food and lodging at the City Mission other than cooperating with staff and addressing the issues that led to a person's homelessness. A willingness to change, or to receive assistance in order to change, is a necessary (and often painful) pre-condition for making progress in one's life.

At a risk of seeming very heartless, the streets, even in a great place to live like Lincoln, are hard and deadly for homeless individuals. Addicts, including alcoholics, die young.

True compassion intervenes in a manner which leads to a viable, long-term solution to the problem. Help, real help, is available at area shelters and drop-in centers. These organizations and their respective staffs address tough issues in the lives of the homeless everyday, and they need support.

The objectives of the People's City Mission are
- To lovingly proclaim the Gospel of Jesus Christ to the economically, emotionally, and spiritually impoverished
- To demonstrate compassion by responding to basic physical and emotional needs
- To promote Christian growth as characterized by a productive, changed life
- To raise the resources of volunteer help, prayer support, financial contributions, in-kind gifts, and long-term follow-up from churches and community

The Mission realizes that people are homeless for a reason and unless those reasons are addressed, the individuals remain homeless.

References

Fradin, D. (1995). From sea to shinning sea Nebraska. Chicago: Children's Press.

Hargrove, J. (1989). America, the beautiful Nebraska. Chicago: Children's Press.

Nebraska. *Encyclopedia americana*. (1986 ed.).

People With Disabilities, Inc., Oasis Lotteries House, 37 Hampden Road, Nedlands .

Website

http://www.city_mission_lincoln.org

http://www.youthservices.com/ysipgms.htm

http://www.jaydn.com/about.html.

CHAPTER 22

The State: New Hampshire

The state of New Hampshire is one of the New England states of the United States. It entered the union on June 21, 1788 as the ninth of the original 13 states. Manchester is the largest city. New Hampshire is known as the **Granite State** because of its extensive granite deposits.

According to the 1990 census, New Hampshire had 1,109,259 inhabitants. Whites made up 98 percent of the population and blacks, 0.6 percent; additional population groups included 2,075 Native Americans, 2,314 people of Chinese origin. Approximately 11,300 people are of Hispanic origin. Roman Catholics form the largest religious group, followed by Methodists, Baptists, Episcopalians, and Presbyterians.

New Hampshire and its people have played important roles in United States history. One of the country's first tax-supported public libraries was established at Peterborough in 1833. In 1853, Franklin Pierce of Hillsboro became the fourteenth President of the United States. In 1961, Alan B. Shepherd of East Derry became the first American to travel in space. Concord's teacher Christa McAulifee was chosen to be the first teacher and first private citizen to fly in a space shuttle mission.

The capital is Concord. The state bird is the purple finch; the state tree, white birch; and the state flower, the purple lilac.

The Person(s)

Governor Jeanne Shaheen

Concord. Governor Jeanne Shaheen is making a difference in the New Hampshire state. Governon Shaheen lives in Madbury with her husband, Bill and their three daughters. Before serving in public office, she managed several statewide campaigns, taught in public schools, and was a small business owner and manager.

As Governor, she made the establishment of statewide incentives for public kindergarten a priority. The legislature passed her plan in 1997, and since then 1,000 additional New Hampshire children have enrolled in public kindergartens. She created the Computers in the Schools initiative to get businesses involved in providing technology to schools. She signed into law a tax-deferred tuition savings plan to help families save for college. She supported important reforms to improve teaching, such as initiating teacher testing and creating a statewide report care on education so that parents and taxpayers can know how their schools measure up.

The Governor has set up various programs in the educational system. Two of her many plans are the ABC Plan and the Pilot Project for Computers in Schools. She visited Franklin Middle School to announce the success of a pilot project involving New Hampshire businesses and the Correctional Industries Program in providing computers for the school at no cost to taxpayers. The Governor spoke to a seventh grade class that is using 24 newly installed, upgraded computers that were donated by businesses and reconstructed by prison inmates.

Another educational plan that the Governor has implemented is the ABC Plan (Advancing Better Classrooms). First, it determines a standard of adequacy for children's education. Second, it establishes a uniform local property tax rate for education and gives supplemental state funds to the towns that need help in providing an adequate education to their students.

The Program(s)

Hampshire County Youth Service

Statewide. The Youth Service creates opportunities throughout the County of Hampshire which encourage young people to achieve their full potential. This is achieved through an educational approach which challenges young people to respond critically and creatively to their everyday experiences and to the wider world around them.

Young people become involved in the Youth Service because they choose to do so by being attracted to the range of opportunities offered. In constructing a learning curriculum, particular emphasis is placed on identifying and connecting with young peoples' own starting points and motivating them to learn is an essential part of the process. A coordinated and progressive range of opportunities are offered which are accessible and based on the principles of equity and fairness. And of course, youth work offers fun social events, leisure, and outdoor activities that excite and challenge young people to make the most of their lives.

By being encouraged to take ownership of their development as essential outcome for young people is the development of self-esteem, awareness, confidence, as well as a range of new skills.

The Youth Service is a part of the County Education Service with six areas which focus on District and Borough Council boundaries. The area teams have a delegated budget and establish an action plan responsive to local needs in keeping county objectives and priorities. Some of the services provided are Duke of Edinburg's Award Scheme; information, advice and counseling; detached and outreach projects; youth clubs and centers; voluntary youth work; and working with the disadvantaged.

References

New Hampshire. *World book encyclopedia.* (1996 ed.).

State of New Hampshire, Office of the Governor, State House, Concord, New Hampshire.

Website

Hanatsweb@hants.gov.uk

CHAPTER 23

The State: New Jersey

The state of New Jersey is one of the Middle Atlantic states of the United States. It entered the union on December 18, 1787 as the third of the original 13 states. Newark is the largest city. New Jersey is known as the **Garden State**.

According to the 1990 census, New Jersey had 7,730,188 inhabitants. Whites made up 79.3 percent of the population and blacks, 13.1 percent; additional population groups included 14,500 Native Americans, 59,084 people of Chinese origin, 79,440 people of Indian origin, 53,146 people of Filipino origin, 38,540 people of Korean origin, 17,257 people of Japanese origin. Approximately 73,900 people are of Hispanic origin. Roman Catholics form the largest religious group, followed by Baptists, Methodists, and Jews.

New Jersey has a rich history and many great people are affiliated with the state. The famous Ivy League, Princeton University, is located in Princeton, New Jersey. George Washington crossed the Delaware to New Jersey. Albert Einstein studied in New Jersey for a short period. Thomas Edison invented the electric light bulb and photograph in New Jersey. Samuel F. B. Morse developed the successful U. S. telegraph near Morristown, New Jersey. Famous singer Whitney Houston is from New Jersey.

The capital is Trenton. The state bird is the willow goldfinch; the state tree, red oak; and the state flower, the purple violet.

The Person(s)

Mr. David Wiesner

Bridgewater. Mr. David Wiesner is a native of Bridgewater, New Jersey. He became interested in art when he was a young child. He grew up in a large family and while growing up, he could recall looking at the wallpaper in his room of eleven years. The wall had stimulating patterns of rockets, magnifying glasses, elephant heads, ships in bottles, books, and medals. The wall, along with the help of his siblings, gave him the aspiration to be an artist. Today, he is a successful artist of children's animated books.

Mr. Wiesner's early artistic education was not just an indoor activity. In fact, whatever familial life did for young David's imagination, it was at least equaled, if not surpassed, by life outside. His Bridgewater neighborhood was one of those perfect places to grow up because it encouraged playing outside. Like his house, but on a much larger scale, the neighborhood had many children of different ages who were involved in different activities. The activities included games according to age groups and other entertaining projects. Mr. Wiesner kept drawing no matter what was going on in the neighborhood.

Mr. Wiesner became familiar with the images of such artists as Da Vinci, Dali, De Chirico, Brueghel, and Durer—all available in the *Time* Books of Great Artists and all contained within the Wiesner home.

In 1983 an apartment fire destroyed all his possessions, including work done up to that time. But it would take more than a fire to stop this smitten bookmaker; *The Loathsome Dragon* (Putman), a story retold by Mr. Wiesner and his surgeon wife Kim Kahng.

With his imagination, skill, and reserve, Mr. Wiesner's passion for making pictures, particularly pictures that tell stories, is clearly evident not only in his books but also in the enthusiasm and sincerity with which he animatedly describes their creation.

Lauryn Hill

South Orange. "Who else can tell my story better than me?" says Lauryn Hill, chanteuse, rapper, songwriter, actress, activist, and mother. She's talking about **The Miseducation of Lauryn Hill** (RuffHouse/Columbia), her solo debut album and one of the most hotly anticipated records of 1998.

Produced by Miss Hill, **The Miseducation of Lauryn Hill** is a deeply personal album, running the gamut from affairs to the heart to socio-political issues, set against a sonic backdrop displaying the remarkable talent of this young native of South Orange, New Jersey. The title, according to Ms. Hill, shouldn't be taken too literally. Ms. Hill explains: "...the concept of 'Miseducation' is not really miseducation at all. To me, it's more or less switching the terminology...it's really about the things that you've learned outside of school, outside of what society deems appropriate and mandatory. I have a lot of respect for academia...But there was a lot that I had to learn—life lessons—that wasn't part of any scholastic curriculum. It's really our passage into adulthood when we leave that place of idealism and naivete."

The Miseducation of Lauryn Hill forays into hip-hop territory with cuts like "Doo Wop" and the Jamaican-tinged grooves of "Lost Ones." Musically, she brings a warmth and sensitivity to the sound of **The Miseducation of Lauryn Hill** and displays her wide knowedge of the workings of the studio as producer on this stunning debut.

Having spent much of her formative years in the nation's spotlight, first as an actress (she appeared in a recurring role in "As the World Turns" and was featured in "Sister Act II: Back In the Habit") and now as a multi-platinum artist who still finds time for charitable causes (she is the founder of non-profit organization, The Refugee Camp Youth Project, whose manifesto is based on giving back to the community and improving the quality of life for inner-city children), Ms. Lauryn Hill has very much come into her own and **The Miseducation of Lauryn Hill** is the musical proof. As Ms. Hill, the hip-hop groundbreaking genius, puts it, "I want my music to touch real people. I'm still trying to figure myself out, like most people...becaue I'm still living and learning..."

The Program(s)

The Refugee Project, Inc.

South Orange. The Refugee Project, Inc., is a non-profit organization founded in 1996 by Columbia Records' recording artist, Lauryn Hill. This organization was founded with the express intent of encouraging positive social action from youth described as "disadvantaged."

The organization's main goal is to remedy the problems of social interaction and to provide positive activities and educational experiences for youth that are often overlooked. The aim is to generate long-term results with consistent, insightful and transformative social programs.

The objective of the project is to transform the lives of young people for the better. The project will change the conversation, agenda, and social fads of youth from negative to positive. It will seek to change the attitudes and social agenda of youth from violence to non-violence, from drugs to sobriety, from miseducation to education, from lack of values and respect to understanding of and appreciation for cultural aesthetics.

Some of the programs include:

- **Camp Hill** is an overnight camp that offers transformative experiences for young people, ages 10-13. Campers enjoy social and recreational activities where the kids build teamwork skills and self-esteem.
- **The Circle Mentoring Program** was created to provide a crucial sense of community, support, and protection for the most vulnerable group susceptible to breaking circles—our children.
- **The Book Worms Reading Club** was created as a reading initiative of the Refugee Project, to address the issue of novice reading. Reading sparks the imagination, adventure, and discovery.

♦ ♦ ♦
References

Ewey, M. (1998, November). Lauryn Hill. E*bony,* pp. 194-197.

Macaulay, D. (1992, July/August). David Wiesner. *The Horn Book Magazine*, pp. 423-428.

New Jersey. *World book encyclopedia.* (1986 ed.).

Sinclair, T. (1998, October). Hill power. *Entertainment*, pp. 28-31.

Websites

http://www.refugeeproject.com

http://www.aft.org

http://www.wipn.state.com

CHAPTER 24

The State: New Mexico

The state of New Mexico is one of the Mountain states of the United States. It entered the union on January 6, 1912 as the forty-seventh state. Albuquerque is the largest city. New Mexico is known as the **Land of Enchantment**.

The region north of Mexico was named Nuevo Mexico by a Spanish explorer in the 1560s. The name was translated and applied to the United States territory organized in 1850 and later to the state. It is bounded on the north by Colorado, and on the east by Oklahoma and Texas.

According to the 1990 census, New Mexico had 1,515,069 inhabitants. Whites made up 75.6 percent of the population and blacks, 2 percent; additional population group included 134,100 Native Americans. Approximately 579,200 people are of Hispanic origin. Roman Catholics form the largest religious group, followed by Baptists, and Methodists.

Visitors are attracted not only by the scenic beauty of New Mexico's deserts and mountains, but also by the rich Native American and Spanish cultural heritage that distinguishes the state. The Palace of Governors, located in Santa Fe, is the oldest government building in the United States.

The capital is Sante Fe. The state bird is the roadrunner; the state tree, pinyon pine; and the state flower, the yucca.

The Person(s)

Mr. Martin J. Chavez

Albuquerque. Mr. Martin J. Chavez is a native of Albuquerque, New Mexico. He earned a bachelor's degree from the University of New Mexico and a law degree from Georgetown University in Washington, D.C. In 1986, Mr. Chavez served as the first director of New Mexico's State Workers' Compensation Administration. He served in the New Mexico State Senate from 1989 to 1993, where he sponsored numerous bills, including legislation for campaign and governmental ethics reform. He was the mayor of Albuquerque, New Mexico from 1993 to 1997. Despite an overwhelming approval rate of 62 to 75 percent, Mr. Chavez decided to run for governor of New Mexico instead of re-election of Albuquerque. Mr. Chavez is married to Margaret Aragon de Chavez, a former school teacher and principal, and they have two young boys.

Mr. Chavez is a person who is concerned about the youth in New Mexico and the overall outlook of youth by others. He is aware that the raising of a student takes place in the school, home, and community. This was shown when as mayor, he pushed initiatives to reduce crime, crack down on gang violence, clean up graffiti, and strengthen the city's partnership with the public schools. He realized that the youth are a generation at risk, and that punishment alone will not solve the problems of youth crime. He understood that in order to stop children from committing serious crimes, they need to be punished for the minor crimes that they commit and not just get a slap on the wrist.

He realized that an idle teen often gets into trouble. As a result, Mr. Chavez challenged local businesses to hire a teen for the summer. The teens went through resume writing and interview technique workshops to help prepare to get a desired job. Consequently, more teenagers were hired into the private sector, more than the federal monies would have allowed. There was a significant reduction in crime.

The Program(s)

Little Kids, Big Projects

Cuba. At Cuba Elementary School in Cuba, New Mexico, you're more likely to hear the rhythmic clackety-clack of young children turning out sophisticated projects on school PCs, than the pulsating beat of a Latin tempo. This is especially true in Debra Gurule's multi-age K-1 classroom. Last year, in a thematic unit on winter, her students used Microsoft PowerPoint to produce online computer books. The project also involved a scanner, a digital camera, and the spreadsheet component of Microsoft Works.

The unit on winter integrated several subject areas. After students read and compared several versions of "The Mitten," a popular Ukrainian folktale, they digitized the cover of each story. After scanning the covers, students used them for display purposes and voted for their favorite by going up to the board and placing a check mark on a printed chart. They transferred the results to a simple spreadsheet. Students clicked on the chart icon to graph the data, experimenting with bar graph and pie chart styles until they found one they thought best represented the data.

The Title I reading/language arts classroom at Marshall Elementary School in Lewisburg, Tennessee, is rich in the use of techonology—which includes 12 powerful Macintosh computers, one large-screen TV, one VCR, two flatbed scanners, CD-Recordable drive, a Quick Take digital camera, ISDN Internet access on all computers, plus Connectix QuickCam video cameras—helps first- and second-graders learn to read. The second grade class uses the Davidson's Multimedia Workshop for online story presentations. They first write their stories on paper. After the teacher reads over their work and helps them with corrections, they take their revised stories to the computer.

Other schools who participated with Microsoft Corporation are Lummis Elementary, K-5 (LasVegas, Nevada) and St. John the Baptist, K-8 (Portland, Oregon).

♦ ♦ ♦

References

Holzberg, C. (1997, October). Little kids, big projects. *Technology and Learning*, 18, pp. 42-47.

New Mexico. *World book encyclopedia.* (1996 ed.).

Website

http://www.martinchavez98.org

CHAPTER 25

The State: New York

The state of New York is one of the Middle Atlantic states of the United States. It entered the union on July 26, 1788 as the eleventh of the 13 original states. New York City is the largest city. New York is known as the **Empire State**.

According to the 1990 census, New York had 17,990,455 inhabitants. Whites made up 74.4 percent of the population and blacks, 15.9 percent (more blacks--2.9 million--live in New York than in any other state); additional population groups included 60,855 Native Americans, 284,144 people of Chinese origin, 140,985 people of Indian origin, 95,648 people of Korean origin, 62,259 people of Filipino origin, and 35,281 people of Japanese origin. Approximately 2.2 million state residents are of Hispanic origin. Roman Catholics form the largest religious group, followed by Baptists, Methodists, Lutherans, Presbyterians, and Episcopalians.

New York City plays host to many extravagant events and is the headquarters of the United Nations. One of the tallest buildings in the world, the Empire State Building, is there along with the World Trade Center. New York is a fashion capital. It is a treasure to all who visit and reside there.

The capital is Albany. The state bird is the bluebird; the state tree, sugar maple; and the state flower, the rose.

The Person(s)

Dr. Antonio Pantoja

Manhattan. Dr. Antonio Pantoja is founder of the ASPIRA Association, Inc. ASPIRA takes its name from the Spanish verb *aspirar*, "aspire."

Dr. Pantoja was born in San Juan, Puerto Rico and studied at the University of Puerto Rico where she obtained a Normal School Diploma in 1942. Upon graduating from the University of Puerto Rico, she worked as a school teacher for two years in Puerto Rico where she cultivated a profound interest in education and addressing the needs of disadvantaged children. She arrived in New York City in November 1944 where she got a job as a welder in a factory making lamps for children.

During these years which involved long hours of hard work, Dr. Pantoja was awakened to the harsh experience of racism and discrimination against Puerto Ricans and how this community lacked the knowledge and political power to overcome these and other challenges in the United States. She became an activist in the factory, providing information to other workers about their rights and how to organize a union. These were the most formative years of her life. But within a few years, the women who welded pieces of filament for submarine radios would rise to weld together a fragmented community, a community much in need of leadership and vision.

Her most profound contribution to the Puerto Rican community in the United States began in 1958 when she joined a group of young professional in creating the Puerto Rican Forum, Inc., which paved the way for the establishment of ASPIRA. Her most notable contribution—the creation of ASPIRA in 1961, was the result of considerable hard work and collaboration with educators and social work professionals who shared her concern with the high dropout rate of Puerto Rican youth in New York City during the '50s and '60s. The organization empowers Puerto Rican youth to have a say in and control of their future.

The Program(s)

The ASPIRA Association, Inc.

New York City. The ASPIRA Association, Inc., is the only national non-profit organization devoted solely to the education and leadership development of Puerto Rican and other Latino youth.

Since 1961 ASPIRA has pursued its mission of empowering the Latino community through the development of its youth. All of ASPIRA's goals and activities spring from one basic belief: Puerto Ricans and Latinos have the collective potential to move their community forward.

ASPIRA looks at Latino youth and sees this potential: Leaders waiting to emerge. With community-based offices in large cities of six states and Puerto Rico, ASPIRA's 500 staff members work with over 25,000 youth and their families each year to develop that potential. The organization refers to them as *Aspirantes*—those youth who will become educated, committed leaders for the community's future benefit.

ASPIRA's mission statement promotes the empowerment of the Puerto Rican and Latino community by developing and nurturing the leadership, intellectual, and cultural potential of its youth so that they may contribute their skills and dedication to the fullest development of the Puerto Rican and Latino community everywhere.

In the last three decades, ASPIRA has become an inclusive organization. While still mainly a Puerto Rican organization, it now reaches out to include all Latinos and a significant group of non-Latinos throughout the United States. Presently, ASPIRA serves over 25,000 students each year in over 400 schools, through its core activity, the ASPIRA Clubs. ASPIRA provides leadership training, career and college counseling, financial aid, scholarship assistance, educational advocacy, cultural activities, and most importantly, continuing opportunities to implement community action projects.

All programs are aimed at helping Latino youth.

♦ ♦ ♦

References

New York. *World book encyclopedia.* (1996 ed.).

Website

http://www.aspira.org/about_assoc.htm

CHAPTER 26

The State: Pennsylvania

The state of Pennsylvania is one of the Middle Atlantic states of the United States. It entered the union on December 12, 1787 as the second of the 13 original states. Philadelphia is the largest city. Pennsylvania is known as the **Keystone State** because of its central location amidst the original 13 states of the union. In 1681, William Penn received a new colony from England's King Charles II. Penn then named his new colony in honor of his father.

According to the 1990 census, Pennsylvania had 11,881,643 inhabitants. Whites made up 88.5 percent of the population and blacks, 9.2 percent; additional population groups included 14,210 Native Americans, 29,562 people of Chinese origin, 28,396 people of Indian origin, 26,787 people of Korean origin, 12,160 people of Filipino origin, and 6,613 people of Japanese origin. Approximately 232,300 state residents are of Hispanic origin. Roman Catholics form the largest religious group, followed by Baptists, Methodists, Lutherans, and Presbyterians.

Pennsylvania played a central role in the birth of the United States; both the Declaration of Independence and the United States Constitution were drawn up and signed in Philadelphia. The state has a substantial Jewish community and is one of the principal centers of the Society of Friends (Quakers).

The capital is Harrisburg. The state bird is the ruffed grouse; the state tree, western hemlock; and the state flower, the mountain laurel.

The Person(s)

Mr. Curtis Martin

Pittsburgh. Thanksgiving may be over, but the spirit of the holidays remains in full force as evidenced by a tractor trailer full of food and one of Pittsburgh's favorite sons.

Pittsburgh native and New York Jets running back Curtis Martin escorted a tractor trailer hauling more than 90 boxes of food to Homewood, where the Feed The Children Program made its latest in a long line of stops across the country.

Feed The Children is an initiative that provides physical, spiritual, educational, vocational, technical, psychological, economic, medical and other assistance to needy children and their families.

Begun in 1979, Feed The Children operates in all 50 states, the District of Columbia and 75 countries worldwide. Since its founding, the organization has distributed more than 400 million pounds of food, clothing, and other necessities.

Last year, Feed The Children helped supplement 340,000 meals daily and distributed 55 million pounds of food and supplies, 80 percent of which remained in the United States. "My purpose is to teach and reveal goodness to the hearts of people by using the talents and gifts I have been blessed with as a vehicle to attain my goal," Mr. Martin said.

The food will be distributed through Martin's church, Faith Restoration Ministries in Homewood and other agencies that help children and families in their struggle with hunger. Items distributed included canned vegetables, cereal, oatmeal, rice, soup, pasta, beans, baby food, crackers and beverages. Feed The Children's partners include Allen Canning Company, Quaker, General Mills, Uncle Ben's, Lipton, Smuckers, Ragu, Wishbone, and Right Guard. "We must address America's hunger problem in which nearly 15 million children struggle with hunger," says Mr. Martin.

The Program(s)

Creating a Caring Community in Classrooms

Indiana. Charlotte M. Krall, partnership liaison for Training and Development, The Southwestern Pennsylvania Connection, and Mary Renck Jalongo, professor, Department of Professional Studies in Education, Indiana University of Pennsylvania, Indiana, Pennsylvania, are the creators of this wonderful idea for students in the classroom.

After spending thousands of hours teaching, observing, and listening to teachers and children in and out of classrooms, they feel that it is important for educators to

- **Be honest. Build mutual trust.** Children need to know where they stand. They need to understand the rules and anticipate reasonable consequences for transgressions. Being honest and building trust doesn't mean the teacher or the child must be totally open at all times.
- **Cultivate communication skills. Be a role model.** When developing classroom communication skills, it is important to be non-judgmental and respect each child's right to privacy and self-preservation. As you interact with students, state your expectations clearly and react to how a child behaves. Body language and tone of voice are particularly powerful means of communication.
- **Adjust the schedule. Be flexible.** When a child shows signs of unbearable or unmanageable frustration; i.e., crying, screaming, trying to run away, or just giving up, schedule adjustments that may help that child regain control.
- **Be human.** Promote humor. Caring teachers pay attention to beginnings, endings, and transitions. They draw the children gently into the school day and help ease them back into the world outside. As a teacher works toward the goal of creating a caring community in his classroom, keep the over-arching purpose of education uppermost in mind.

♦ ♦ ♦

References

Jalongo, M., & Krall, C. (1998/99, Winter). Creating a caring community in classrooms. *Childhood Education,* 74, pp. 83-88.

Pennsylvania. *World book encyclopedia.* (1994 ed.).

Website

http://www.feedthechildren.org

CHAPTER 27

The State: Rhode Island

The state of Rhode Island is one of the New England states of the United States. It entered the union on May 29, 1790 as the last of the 13 original states. Providence is the largest city. Rhode Island is known as the **Ocean State**.

According to the 1990 census, Rhode Island had 1,003,464 inhabitants. Whites made up 91.4 percent of the population and blacks, 3.9 percent; additional population groups included 3,987 Native Americans, 3,170 people of Chinese origin, 2,579 people of Laotian origin, and 3,655 people of Cambodian origin. Approximately 45,000 state residents are of Hispanic origin. Roman Catholics form the largest religious group, followed by Baptists, Episcopalians, and Methodists.

Rhode Island lies on beautiful Narragansett Bay, an arm of the Atlantic Ocean. The bay makes the state a leading vacation land and an important defense center. The state has 36 islands, most of which are in the bay. Aquidneck, the largest island, was officially named Rhode Island in 1644. Towns on the mainland were called Providence Plantation. As a result, Rhode Island's official name is State of Rhode Island and Providence Plantations. Thus, the smallest state has the longest official name.

The capital is Providence. The state bird is the Rhode Island red; the state tree, red maple; and the state flower, the purple violet.

The Person(s)

Mrs. Leona A. Kelly

Peace Dale. Mrs. Leona A. Kelly is a state representative for the state of Rhode Island. Mrs. Kelly is a native of Providence, Rhode Island and presently resides in Peace Dale, Rhode Island. She is married to Mr. Milton A. Kelly and they have two children.

Mrs. Kelly has had an exceptional education which stems from an undergraduate degree which she received from the University of Rhode Island in 1941. She has also received master degrees from the University of Rhode Island, Rhode Island College, and Bryan Mawr.

While attending college, Mrs. Kelly held quite a few occupations. After receiving her undergraduate degree, she worked as a social worker for a couple of years and had a great impact on many lives. But the field in which Mrs. Kelly had the greatest impact was as an educator.

As a teacher, she had an opportunity to exemplify skillful tactics in furnishing the students with a formal education. Although she enjoyed teaching, she wanted to do more. Mrs. Kelly decided to take up politics and also dedicated herself to the betterment of her society. Mrs. Kelly formed and belongs to many organizations, which are designed to provide services to those in need.

Her main focus is solely based on the educational system. She is a profound member of the

- Cane Educational Center
- 4-H Foundation Rhode Island
- Retired Teachers Association
- The Study Commission on Women's Health Issues

Mrs. Kelly has made extraordinary contributions which have, in turn, helped many individuals. Mrs. Kelly is of Anglo-Irish decent.

The Program(s)

Rhode Island's Interactive Science Museum

Providence. There is no place in Rhode Island or anywhere in the United States in which kids can crawl through and examine a city sewer system while their parents look on. But there will be one in October.

The residents of Providence, the capital of Rhode Island, got together and through a fund raising project raised $3 million to modify an old museum into an interactive extravaganza which, unlike an ordinary museum, will allow kids to view and have a hands-on learning experience. Many experts and planners believe that individuals will learn the information displayed better than if they browsed and read abstracts.

The first interactive exhibit will contain large mirrors and lenses. These items play an important role because they show the kids that learning can be fun and that's really important when it comes to kids.

The next exhibit teaches the kids about waterways. It focuses on the way waterways move. The kids have an opportunity to build their own fountain and create different channels for water to flow through in a big tank.

The third interactive activities for the children are pets and people. Kids will have fun learning about different homes for animals and how to take care of their pets. The Animal Rescue League has teamed up to help with this project. One of the most ambiguous learning experiences that the youth will experience will be a computerized interactive history tunnel.

This exhibit will allow the kids to hear and actually converse with computerized individuals of different ethnic groups. The exhibit focuses on teaching kids the history of different ethnic groups who migrated to the United States.

The Museum focuses on the education of all. The ethnic make up of the program contains members of the community, which stem from every walk of life.

References

Allen, G. (1978). *Rhode Island*. New Jersey: Prentice-Hall.

Arnold, J. (1950). *The history of Rhode Island*. Providence: Historical Publishing, Company.

Bartlett, J. (1970). *Bibliography of Rhode Island*. Rhode Island: Providence Printing Company.

Cady, J. (1986). *Rhode Island boundaries*. Providence: Rhode Island Press.

McGraw, J. (1999). *The Rhode Island parents' paper*. Portsmouth: Rhode Island Press.

Rhode Island. *World book encyclopedia*. (1994 ed.).

Website

http://www.family.go.com

CHAPTER 28

The State: South Carolina

The state of South Carolina is one of the South Atlantic states of the United States. It entered the union on May 23, 1788 as the eighth of the 13 original states. Columbia is the largest city. South Carolina is known as the **Palmetto State** because of the many palmetto trees that grow there. South Carolina is the only gold-producing state east of the Mississippi River.

According to the 1990 census, South Carolina had 3,486,703 inhabitants. Whites made up 69 percent of the population and blacks, 29.8 percent; additional population groups included 8,050 Native Americans (many of whom are members of the Catawba group), 3,039 people of Chinese origin, 3,900 people of Indian origin, 2,577 people of Korean origin, 5,521 people of Filipino origin, 1,885 people of Japanese, and 1,752 people of Vietnamese origin. Approximately 30,550 state residents are of Hispanic origin. Baptists form the largest religious group, followed by Methodists, Roman Catholics, Presbyterians, and Episcopalians.

Over 200 battles and skirmishes occurred in the state. South Carolina was the first state to secede from the union when it ratified the Ordinance of Secession in 1860. The first shots of the Civil War were fired at Fort Sumter (Charleston).

The capital is Columbia. The state bird is the Carolina wren; the state tree, palmetto; and the state flower, the yellow jessamine.

The Person(s)

Senator Maggie Wallace Glover

Florence. Senator Maggie Wallace Glover, Democrat, District Number 30, Florence-Marion-Dillon Counties, is an African American educator, residing in Florence. She graduated from Fayetteville State University, B.A., 1970; Francis Marion College, M.Ed., 1982. She is a member of the Florence School District I; School Board of Trustees, 1983-86; re-elected 1986-89; Children's Theater; director of Bushua Arts Foundation, 1982; Order of the Palmetto, 1993; Executive Commissioner of the Florence Branch NAACP; military service, United States Army, 1974-77; previously served in the House 1989-92; and the Senate 1993-97.

Senator Glover is a strong advocate for children with special needs. As a senator, she sponsored bills that provided for the special need students. A description of Section 59-33-116, Section 1, 1976 Amended Code by the Assembly of the State of Carolina follows.

> Assistive technology means a device of service which is used to increase, maintain, or improve the functional capacities of an individual with a disability. An assistive technology device is an item, piece of equipment, or product system, whether acquired commercially, off the shelf, modified, or customized that is used to increase, maintain, or improve the function capacities of an individual with disability including, but not limited to, aids for daily living, augmentative communication devices, wheelchairs, and mobility aids, seating and position aids, computer aids, environmental controls, home and workplace modification, prosthetics and orthotics, or aids for vision or hearing impairments. An assistive technology service is a service that directly assists an individual with a disability in the selection, acquisition, or use of an assistive technology device.

Senator Glover continuously works hard daily for the many causes she endorses.

The Program(s)

South Carolina Higher Education Tuition Grants

Statewide. The **Tuition Grants Program** is administered by the South Carolina Higher Education Tuition Grants Commission and is made possible through an annual appropriation by the South Carolina General Assemby. The purpose of the program is to provide undergraduate grant assistance to eligible South Carolina residents attending, on a full-time basis, certain independent non-profit colleges located in the state.

Just as the state of South Carolina offsets the cost of all students who attend the state's public colleges, the Legislature felt it would be equitable to assist those eligible South Carolinians who prefer to attend one of South Carolina's twenty participating independent colleges.

Application for a South Carolina Tuition Grant is made by completing the Free Application for Federal Student Aid (FAFSA). The FAFSA is available at all South Carolina high schools, colleges, and the South Carolina Tuition Grants Commission. By submitting the FAFSA to the federal government's processor and by listing the South Carolina independent college of the student's choice in the college choice section, the Tuition Grants Commission will be able to electronically receive the application from the federal processor. The Commission will then use the student's application information to compute his South Carolina Tuition Grant eligibility. Also, since South Carolina Tuition Grants are available only to legal residents of South Carolina, it is necessary to accurately complete all questions on the FAFSA regarding state residency.

Financial factors used to determine eligibility are (1) family income, (2) family assets, (3) cost of the college selected, (4) number of family members in the household, and (5) the number of household members attending college. Students do not have to repay the grant. However, if they drop out of school, the unused portion of the grant must be refunded to the state.

♦ ♦ ♦

References

Senator Maggie Wallace Glover, 504 Gresette Building, Columbia, South Carolina.

South Carolina. *World book encyclopedia.* (1996 ed.).

Website

http://www.state.sc.us/tuitiongrants

CHAPTER 29

The State: South Dakota

The state of South Dakota is one of the West North Central states of the United States. It entered the union on November 2, 1889 as the fortieth state. Sioux City is the largest city. South Dakota is known as the **Coyote State** after South Dakota's state animal, and the **Sunshine State**, which is a promotional name used to attract tourists.

According to the 1990 census, South Carolina had 696,004 inhabitants. Whites made up 91.6 percent of the population and blacks, 0.5 percent; additional population groups included 50,500 Native Americans (the Sioux form the largest Native American group in the state), 385 people of Chinese origin, 525 people of Korean origin, 531 people of Filipino origin, 286 people of Japanese, and 287 people of Indian origin. Approximately 5,250 state residents are of Hispanic origin. Lutherans form the largest religious group, followed by Roman Catholics, Methodists, Baptists, and Presbyterians.

Farms and ranches cover about nine-tenths of the state. Sheep and cattle graze on the sprawling ranches of the western plains and on smaller farms in the east. Some influential people who evolved South Dakota into what it is today include such names as Calamity Jane, Sitting Bull, and Wild Bill Hickcock.

The capital is Pierre. The state bird is the ring-necked pheasant; the state tree, black hills spruce; and the state flower, the American pasque.

The Person(s)

Ms. Judith E. Kroll

Brookings. For over thirty years, Mrs. Judith E. Kroll has enriched the educational fabric of a small rural community in Brookings, South Dakota. At the conclusion of her current school term, Ms. Kroll emphasized "how vital the role of teaching is to our nation's future."

Ms. Kroll has exemplified what a life-long commitment to education and the future of students can mean for a community. She shows people that education is about understanding--teachers understanding kids; kids understanding kids; and the community members understanding one another.

In her years of teaching at Brookings High School, Ms. Kroll has seen her community evolve to one that is no longer white, as middle class, or as conservative. In 1995, more people in her community worked on farms than processing plants. The students in her history, literature, humanities, and writing classes may come with English as second or unfamiliar languages. She teaches in a community and in a school that are struggling to redefine themselves for the 21st Century. The walls of this extraordinary teacher's room are covered with posters featuring pioneers of the past to entrepreneurs and modern candid shots of life in school.

Ms. Kroll states, "It's when kids and I work together that something happens—ideas take shape." The goal is to expose kids to a multitude of ideas and situations while asking them to connect, create, and analyze. One of the biggest challenges that education now faces is how to make school meaningful and relevant to all students.

Her philosophy of teaching has evolved over the course of her career to encompass more of the "why" and "how" of learning. "Present and prospective educators are here to serve the needs of the students, not awaken our students to our own truths," says Ms. Kroll.

SOUTH DAKOTA

Governor William J. Janklow

Statewide. Governor William J. Janklow has won more cases in the United States Supreme Court than any lawyer in Dakota's history. Some of his many achievements include

- Cracked down on welfare fraud, drug abuse, and white collar crime
- Upgraded the state crime lab
- Accelerated the transfer of children from foster care to adoption
- Kept his campaign promise of "Putting Taxpayers First"
- Reduced the state government bureaucracy by almost ten percent
- Prevented the budget crisis that occurred in over 30 other states in seeing it coming and reducing state spending the previous August
- Created more new plant expansions, more new industries and capital investment in South Dakota in his eight years than had been in the previous twelve years at a time when federal policies were record-breaking years of high interest rates and inflation
- Creatively used prison labor for state fairgrounds rebuilding and other projects
- Implemented a rural renaissance program and computerized farm management course
- Transformed a small state college campus into a prison
- Stopped the atmosphere of violence tremendously

Governor Janklow made state government more efficient by managing it like business and has re-negotiated state contracts to make them less costly to the taxpayer, promoted joint ventures with city and county governments to prevent local increases and eliminated over sixty state government newsletters.

At the end of his eight years as governor, one citizen told the Tribune, "We need someone as outspoken and animated as Janklow." State Senator George Shanard told a newspaper that Janklow's "extra aggressive, extremely intelligent. He's probably regarded of the best—if not the best—governors in South Dakota history."

The Program(s)

Alcohol Free Kids

Sioux City. Alcohol Free Kids is a program in Sioux City, South Dakota. The program was started by Sandy Golden in 1997 to mobilize a grassroots movement against underage drinking and drunk driving.

The program began when its creator started touring South Dakota and Iowa, talking about underage drinking and drunk driving. Ms. Golden started out as an investigative reporter working on a story about the topic and said the topic exploded across the United States about nineteen years ago. Since that time, several programs have been formed and many were based on a book written by Ms. Golden entitled, *How to Save Lives and Reduce Injuries*. From the beginning, Ms. Golden did not have the money to teach kids across the world. But with computer technology and internal access that has changed.

The goals of Alcohol Free Kids are
- Teaching teens and college students how to organize on the issue of drunk driving
- Forming emergency action teams at the local level

Alcohol Free Kids teaches volunteers how to inform the public of the problem, how to work for increased enforcement, how to evaluate the current system, and identify areas that need change. Such master planning at the community level is a main component of the Alcohol Free Kids' solution to underage drinking and drunk driving.

"Young people have a tremendous amount of power if someone takes the time to teach them how to use it," says Ms. Golden. Alcohol Free Kids is working toward getting a congressional hearing on uniform standards of drunk driving control and a presidential commission on underage drinking.

A growing number of people are taking notes and listening to what is being said.

SOUTH DAKOTA

HUD Block Funds

Clay County. Clay County has applied for a $200,000 annual **HUD Block Fund**. Presently, the Rural and Remote Community Fairness Act, introduced by Sen. Tom Daschle (D-SD), sets aside $50 million in block grants. The money is reserved for rural counties and Indian tribes suffering severe population losses and low per capita income levels.

An estimated 200 counties and tribes—including seventeen from South Dakota—will qualify nationwide for the Housing and Urban Development (HUD) funds. "The money will help bridge the growing gap between rural and urban areas," Daschle said. He noted, for example, agriculture has been hit hard by shrinking exports, disaster, and other outside forces.

Ironically, Clay County was recently recognized for its population, sales tax and job growth this decade. Clay County's success is part of a boom throughout the region. However, Clay County meets the United States Department of Agriculture's (USDA) criteria for Daschle's program. In order to qualify for the funding, counties or Indian reservations must have out-migration levels of at least one percent over a five-year period; per capita income levels below national averages; borders that are not adjacent to metropolitan areas; and cities with populations less than 15,000.

According to USDA figures, Clay County recorded an out-migration rate of 3.48 percent for 1993-98. The county's average 1996 income was $15,749 per capita, which is below the national average. In addition, the county does not lie near metro areas. Vermillion, its largest city, has about 10,000 residents.

The program runs through 2006, when it would come up for re-authorization. While the bill has just started its journey through Congress, the legislation offers numerous possibilities for South Dakota's rural areas based on the criteria for application. Clay Country meets the criteria. These areas are in dire need of funding.

References

Carpenter, A. (1978). *The enchantment of America: South Dakota*. Chicago: Children's Press.

South Dakota. *World book encyclopedia*. (1996 ed.).

Thompson, K. (1987). *Portrait of America: South Dakota*. Chicago: Raintree Publishers.

Website

http://www.state.sd.us/governor/biography.htm

http://develop.eesso.cybercentral.com/ntoy96.htm

CHAPTER 30

The State: Tennessee

The state of Tennessee is one of the East South Central states of the United States. It entered the union on June 1, 1796 as the sixteenth state. Memphis is the largest city. Tennessee is known as the **Volunteer State**.

According to the 1990 census, Tennessee had 4,877,185 inhabitants. Whites made up 83 percent of the population and blacks, 16 percent; additional population groups included 9,859 Native Americans, 5,653 people of Chinese origin, 4,508 people of Korean origin, 3,032 people of Filipino origin, 3,440 people of Japanese, 5,911 people of Indian origin, and 2,062 people of Vietnamese origin. Approximately 32,700 state residents are of Hispanic origin. Baptists form the single largest religious group, followed by Methodists, Roman Catholics, Presbyterians, and Pentecostals.

Some famous places include Beale Street Historical District, where blues music was developed in the early 20th Century; Graceland, the home of singer Elvis Presley; the nightclub of the "King of the Blues," B. B. King; and Lorraine Motel, the place where Dr. Martin Luther King, Jr., was slain. Historical houses include the homes of President James K. Polk (Columbia), President Andrew Jackson (Hermitage), and President Andrew Johnson (Greeneville).

The capital is Nashville. The state bird is the mockingbird; the state tree, tulip-poplar; and the state flower, the iris.

The Person(s)

Dr. Elizabeth Swartz

Old Hickory. Dr. Elizabeth Swartz is presently educational consultant where she has an internationally recognized program. She further serves as staff developer in the areas of authentic assessment, block scheduling, cooperative learning, integrating the curriculum, multiple intelligences theory, strategic and tactical planning.

Her long list of achievements include:

- **Phi Delta Kappa/International Renewal Institute Program Coordinator of the Network of Mindful Schools**. Coordinated and directed a national network of schools committed to educational reform including helping each school design its own tactical plan for change, providing on-going on-site training, and conducting on-going evaluation of each school's tactical plan.
- **Education Consultant to the Superintendent of Education, Indiana Department of Education**. Charged to create values-oriented community programs which involved school-age youth. In the first program year, fourteen communities across Indiana initiated values awareness programs.
- **Director of Special Projects, Tennessee State Department of Education**. Coordinated Tennessee's "Teacher of the Year" program. Implemented significant changes in the evaluation procedures. Packaged 1987 Tennessee "Teacher of the Year" national program; helped develop and implement statewide Tennessee's mandated child sexual abuse prevention curriculum in conjunction with the Tennessee Department of Human Resources; wrote the superintendent's manual for evaluating principals/supervisors for Tennessee's Career Ladder Program.

Dr. Swartz stated that she always wanted to help the community in every way that she could, especially students.

The Program(s)

Network of Mindful Schools

Old Hickory. The Network of Mindful Schools program is coordinated by Dr. Elizabeth Swartz. It is a national network of schools committed to educational reform. Some of the components of the program include

- Helping each school design its own tactical plan for change
- Providing on-going and on-site training
- Conducting on-going evaluation of each school's tactical plan
- Developing a strategic plan for implementation
- Incorporating new theories of learning with best-practice teaching techniques
- Validating the use of alternative assessment tools with standard practices

The Network of Mindful Schools Program incorporates the strategies needed to create a learner-centered school for the 21st Century. The model also requires a lot of hard work on the part of the teachers and a lot of support from the principal. The principal must participate in all of the in-service sessions so he knows what to expect in the classroom as teacher and students interact.

The components of the "fish bone" represent all the strategies that were shared over a three-year period. Some of the components of a learner-centered school that were listed in the program were cooperative and cognitive, which consist of thinking, writing, pairing, sharing, graphic organizing, and completing jigsaws.

Another is higher order thinking skills, which include metacognition, graphics, three-story intellects, and multiple intelligences consisting of performances, role plays, and demonstrations.

Other components were journals, portfolios, rubrics, thematic units, extended projects, and real-life applications.

◆ ◆ ◆

References

Interview (via Telephone). Dr. Elizabeth Swartz, December 1, 1998.

Tennessee. *World book encyclopedia.* (1996 ed.).

CHAPTER 31

The State: Texas

The state of Texas is one of the West South Central states of the United States. It entered the union on December 29, 1845 as the twenty-eighth state. Houston is the largest city. Texas is known as the **Lone Star State** for the single star on its flag.

According to the 1990 census, Texas had 16,986,510 inhabitants. Whites made up 75.2 percent of the population and blacks, 11.9 percent; additional population groups included 69,349 Native Americans, 63,232 people of Chinese origin, 31,775 people of Korean origin, 34,350 people of Filipino origin, 14,795 people of Japanese, 55,795 people of Indian origin, and 64,634 people of Vietnamese origin. Approximately 4,339,900 state residents are of Hispanic origin. Baptists form the single largest religious group, followed by Roman Catholics, Methodists, Pentecostals, and Lutherans.

The state has the most farms, farmland, cattle, horses, and sheep in the nation. It leads the nation in the production of oil, natural gas, and electrical power. Texas is the greatest source of salt, magnesium, and sulphur. The well-known cities are Houston, with the manned Space Center, Dallas, in the heart of the oil and cotton region, and Austin.

The capital is Austin. The state bird is the mockingbird; the state tree, pecan; and the state flower, the bluebonnet.

The Person(s)

Drs. Joe and Elvia Rodriguez

Nacogdoches. In 1975, the Rodriguezes were contacted by Stephen F. Austin to develop a bilingual program at Stephen F. Austin State University. They visited the campus and fell in love with the heritage rich location of the campus in Deep East Texas. They thought the small city atmosphere would be great for raising their children. They thought it would be the perfect place to begin a career together.

The Rodriguezes joined the Stephen F. Austin faculty and as co-directors of the Title VII program, obtained more than $3 million in federal grants to enhance educational opportunities for teachers preparing to instruct students with limited English proficiency.

The Rodriguezes have been rewarded for their successes. Last year, he was named regents professor, the highest honor awarded faculty at the university. He joined his wife, who received the distinction in 1993, and they became the first married couple to be named regents professors.

The destination carries a $2,000 grant, recognition at commencement, a medal, and reduced teaching assignment during the year of destination. She was honored with the distinction of "Woman of the Year" by the university's "Professional Women at the University" in 1997.

Although they have now won the top honor offered to Stephen F. Austin professors, the Rodriguezes are not ones to sit around basking in their glory. They are still busy in the quest to better the education of teachers, especially bilingual teachers and spent two weeks this summer in Juneau, Alaska, where they presented an international study on gender biases to the National Council of Professors of Educational Administration.

Dr. Joe Rodriguez states: "Fear creates prejudice, a fear of the unknown. So when the unknown becomes known, we will end prejudice. Education is the answer."

The Program(s)

Accelerated Learning Center

Nacogdoches. The **Accelerated Learning Center** is a special school for special young adults with special needs. It is a school of choice, a school of need, but not a school of convenience. It is an alternative school. It is different from the traditional high school. The Accelerated Learning Center is a school designed to assist students to get back on grade level and to obtain their high school diplomas. The work is not easier, but it is different. This difference may make it easier for some students to do their work in order to earn a diploma.

The goal at the Center is to provide an encouraging atmosphere with high expectations for the students. The administrators and teachers at the Center assume all students will display a positive attitude toward the Accelerated Learning Center. If all students will display a positive attitude, neither the student nor staff members will have to be concerned with disciplinary measures. Thus, everyone can concentrate on academic achievement for the benefit of the student body.

The entire instructional program varies from the traditional. The Accelerated Learning Center is centered around a completely individualized program with open entry/open exit. This means a student may enter at any time of the year and complete his/her course of study at any time of the year.

The curriculum is self-paced so that each student works toward mastery and completion of each course. As soon as a student completes a course, a new course is begun. There is no pressure of "being behind" or competing for grades. Each student progresses totally independently of other students. All deadlines are removed. There are no six weeks grading periods, no semesters, no teacher test days. Test days are selected by the student as he/she is ready.

References

Handbook. Accelerated Learning Center, Nacogdoches Independent School District, Nacogdoches, Texas.

Interview. Dr. Elvia Rodriguez, October 10, 1998, Stephen F. Austin University, Nacogdoches, Texas.

Texas. *World book encyclopedia.* (1996 ed.).

CHAPTER 32

The State: Vermont

The state of Vermont is one of the New England states of the United States. It entered the union on March 4, 1791 as the fourteenth state. Burlington is the largest city. Vermont is known as the **Green Mountain State**.

According to the 1990 census, Vermont had 562,758 inhabitants. Whites made up 98.6 percent of the population and blacks, 0.3 percent; additional population groups included 1,650 Native Americans, 679 people of Chinese origin, 563 people of Korean origin, and 529 people of Indian origin. Approximately 3,700 state residents are of Hispanic origin. Roman Catholics form the largest religious group, followed by Methodists and Baptists.

Some interesting tidbits about Vermont: Although Vermont was the first state to prohibit slavery and enact an antislavery resolution, few blacks live there. The most unique aspect of the state is its educational system. The Vermont Constitution of 1777 provided for the establishment of elementary schools in towns and for a grammar school in each county. It is the most topographically diverse of the New England states and is the only one without a seacoast. The Morgan horse is the state's mammal. The honeybee is the state's insect. The state's song is "Hail, Vermont!" by Josephine Hovey Perry.

The capital is Montpelier. The state bird is the hermit thrush; the state tree, sugar maple; and the state flower, the red clover.

The Person(s)

Dr. Susan Brody Hasazi

Burlington. Dr. Susan Brody Hasazi is a Caucasian female of Jewish decent, educated in Burlington, Vermont at a boarding school for girls in the Champlain Valley. With a keen interest in individual rights, she pursued a degree in education. She received her undergraduate degree in 1969 and her master's degree in special education from the University of Vermont in 1972. In 1976 she received her Certificate of Advanced Graduate Study in Administration and Planning from the University of Vermont. She decided to become a part of the University of Vermont because she wanted to give back to the university all that it had given to her. She is currently a professor of education and the director of the University of Vermont's Center on Transition and Employment.

Dr. Hasazi has been widely published and consulted on the transition of youths with disabilities to adults and working life. In June 1995 she received the Joseph P. Kennedy, Jr., Foundation's International Mental Retardation Award in Education. This award was presented to her due to her outstanding contributions to the special education domain. Dr. Hasazi was named one of the four 1996-97 university scholars for her nationally recognized work in special education, and significant contribution in the development of innovative programs and practices which have resulted in remarkable educational outcomes for students with mental retardation.

Under Dr. Hasazi's leadership, Vermont has developed the most inclusive and respected special education systems in the United States. Her work has attracted over $7 million in grants used to improve education and employment options for students with disabilities and the training of graduate students in this particular field. Most recently, she received $1.8 million dollars in grants from the United States Department of Education's Office of Special Education Programs to use for students with disabilities, at age 16, to receive help in planning steps beyond high school.

The Program(s)

I-Team

Burlington. The vision of the Vermont **I-Team** is for every child in Vermont who has significant learning difficulties to feel welcomed in his/her class and community.

The I-Team assists local teams of families, educators, and other service providers in the delivery of quality educational services to students with intensive educational needs through technical assistance, professional development, and family support.

The program serves students residing in Vermont. The student has to meet the eligibility criteria set by the Department of Education for special education services.

The I-Team's services are as vast as its program. The services offered include:
- On-site consultations
- Family support services
- In-service training
- Consultation to related service providers
- Assistance with service delivery planning
- Sharing of current and appropriate literature
- Information and referral sources
- Teaching course work
- Transition planning
- On-going assistance

The members of the I-Team are called upon as needed by the Regional Educational Consultant. These members are usually educators, parents, or other social service professionals.

The program is sponsored by the State Department of Education, University of Vermont's Special Education Department. Its founder is Dr. Susan Brody Hasazi.

♦ ♦ ♦

References

Handbook. State Department of Education, Burlington, Vermont.

Interview (via Telephone). Dr. Susan Brody Hasazi, October 22, 1998, University of Vermont, Burlington, Vermont.

Vermont. *World book encyclopedia.* (1996 ed.).

CHAPTER 33

The State: Virginia

The state of Virginia is one of the South Atlantic states of the United States. It entered the union on June 25, 1788 as the tenth of the original 13 states. Virginia Beach is the largest city. Virginia is known as the **Old Dominion State**.

According to the 1990 census, Virginia had 6,187,358 inhabitants. Whites made up 77.4 percent of the population and blacks, 18.8 percent; additional population groups included 14,893 Native Americans, 21,238 people of Chinese origin, 30,164 people of Korean origin, 20,494 people of Indian origin, 35,067 people of Filipino origin, and 20,693 of Vietnamese origin. Approximately 160,300 state residents are of Hispanic origin. Baptists, Methodists, and Roman Catholics form the largest religious groups.

One of the first English communities in North America was established at Jamestown in 1607, and Virginia subsequently became an important colony. Major battles of the American Revolution and Civil War were fought in the state.

Virginia is famous as the birthplace of many notable Americans, including eight presidents—George Washington, Thomas Jefferson, James Madison, James Monroe, William Henry Harrison, John Tyler, Zachary Taylor, and Woodrow Wilson.

The capital is Richmond. The state bird is the cardinal; the state tree, dogwood; and the state flower, the flowering dogwood.

The Person(s)

Miss Jina Moore

Wheeling. Miss Jina Moore is not only a high school student attending school in Wheeling, West Virginia, but also a high achiever trying to make things happen for young people who are attending Wheeling Park High School.

Miss Moore went to Charleston to speak with Governor Cecil Underwood to explain the work and the mission of the West Virginia Holocaust Education Commission and to enlist his help with this venture.

The conversation with the governor is one more step in the process of establishing a Holocaust educational center for West Virginia students. The story of the Holocaust is not being effectively taught in West Virginia schools.

The commission is working to establish a central location to act as a site for a lending library and to assist with training West Virginia teachers about the history of the Holocaust.

Ms. Moore, the daughter of Tom and Dauna Moore of Wheeling, has been involved with this group for just over a year. She explained that the West Virginia Holocaust Education Committee was founded by Dr. Edith Levy, a former West Virginia University professor and Holocaust survivor originally from Austria, to address the lack of Holocaust teaching at the high school level. Educators and clergy from around the state make up most of the panel's membership.

The local high school senior is the only student member. Miss Moore said she was asked to serve because Dr. Levy knew of her passionate interest in the Holocaust. As the only student member of the non-profit panel, Miss Moore said she finds the commission's work compelling. She has been interested in the Holocaust ever since re-reading *The Diary of Anne Frank*. "I wanted to learn more about the Holocaust and for eight years have studied and read about it in depth," she said.

Mr. Kevin Ward

Roanoke. Mr. Kevin Ward was a black kid who grew up in a non-traditional home. As a teenager he faced many hardships and setbacks. He had been selling crack cocaine only a few weeks before getting caught. Now he was going to face his day in court, and maybe jail, back in his hometown of Roanoke.

Two successful black men, Clayton Bourgess and Ken Belton, worked with Mr. Ward. They knew Mr. Ward was a good kid. He went to church every Sunday. He worked hard at washing cars and mowing lawns. He'd never been in trouble before this. And he was an athlete—he'd been a top lineman the year before on Roanoke's William Fleming High School's football team. He seemed to have little else going for him.

His grades were lousy. He had no hope of getting into college. He'd been diagnosed as learning disabled in elementary school and the tag had stuck with him through the years—on his permanent record and in his own mind.

For people who didn't know what was in his heart, it would have been easy to write him off with all the quick-and-easy labels that so many slap on young black males.

But Ken Belton and Clayton Bourgess knew better. They had hope for Kevin, perhaps more hope at this moment than he had for himself. That's why, on that September morning in 1992, they stayed on his case as he drove toward his destiny.

Six years later, Mr. Kevin Ward is still the same person he ever was; hardworking, attentive around older adults, a big guy with an easy smile. But he has changed, too, and so has his life.

Today, he is a college athlete with pro football aspirations. He has spent countless hours in the weight room, heaping muscles onto his now 300-pound frame. He is an inspirational, sought-after public speaker, equally at ease in a church pulpit or at the front of a school auditorium. He is also a scholar. The young man who was once teased by his schoolmates for being in special education classes is now on the dean's list. Mr. Ward rose from the depths of adversity to the heights of success.

The Program(s)

Healthy Schools

Statewide. Schools working together with families, health care workers, the media, religious organizations, community organizations that serve youth, and young people can address the problems in children's health and social welfare. The program **Healthy Schools** consists of several components that attempt to address the health needs of Kanawha and other county school children. A brief description of each component follows.

- **Health Education**: A planned, sequential K-12 curriculum that addresses the physical, mental, emotional, and social dimensions of health. The curriculum is designed to motivate and assist students to maintain and improve their health, prevent disease, and reduce health-related risk behaviors.

- **Physical Education**: A planned, sequential K-12 curriculum that provides cognitive content and learning experiences in a variety of activity areas such as basic movement skills; physical fitness; rhythms and dance; games, team dual and individual sports; tumbling and gymnastics; and aquatics.

- **Health Services**: Services provided for students to appraise, protect, and promote health. These services are designed to ensure access or referral to primary health care services.

- **Nutrition Services**: Access to a variety of nutritious and appealing meals that accommodate the health and nutrition needs of all students.

- **Counseling and Psychological Services**: Services provided to improve students' mental, emotional, and social health.

- **Parent/Community Involvement**: An integrated school, parent, and community approach for enhancing the health and well-being of students.

Telephone Pioneers

Wheeling. When a child is involved in a traumatic situation, local emergency personnel can comfort a child in need with a soft, huggable bear. The **Telephone Pioneers**, the community service organization of Bell Atlantic West Virginia, is working with schools throughout the state on the Hug-a-Bear campaign. Alice Vandergift and the students at South Junior High School in Morgantown are participating in this community service program.

After the students completed their hug-a-bears, they were donated to the Ohio County Sheriff's Department. The bears were accepted by deputy Ron Meyer of the sheriff's department.

These handmade stuffed bears will now be placed in emergency vehicles to be used in traumatic situations involving a child.

Hug-a-Bear is a community service project initiated by the Telephone Pioneers in 1976. In West Virginia, these 11-inch, soft huggable bears are handmade from fabric donated by Schwab and Company of Creseptown, Maryland, a leading children's clothing manufacturer. In addition, Polymerics Incorporated of Natick, Massachusetts, donates the paint used for the Hug-a Bear face. The Telephone Pioneers provide the stuffing, so the bears can be made at no expense to students. These bears are then donated to local hospitals, law enforcement officers, firefighters, and EMS agencies to help children in traumatic situations.

The purpose of the Telephone Pioneers is to promote and participate in activities that respond to community needs and problems. This volunteer organization has a strong focus on education and is composed of employees and retirees of the United States and Canadian telecommunications industries.

The Telephone Pioneers are encouraging schools to get involved in the Hug-a-Bear program, not only to benefit emergency agencies, but to have a community service learning opportunity that can effectively demonstrate to students how volunteerism can impact a community.

♦ ♦ ♦

References

Interview (via Telephone). Ronald F. Newcome, (February 12, 1999), Community Service Chairman for West Virginia, Route 3, Box 385, Fairmont, West Virginia.

Virginia. *World book encyclopedia*. (1998 ed.).

Wheeling high school student: W. Virginia holocaust resource and education center needed. (1999, March). *The West Virginia News*, p. 1.

Websites

http://www.roanoketimes.com

http://www.ruralnet.marshall.edu/healthy-schools

CHAPTER 34

The State: Wisconsin

The state of Wisconsin is one of the East North Central states of the United States. It entered the union on May 29, 1848 as the thirtieth state. Milwaukee is the largest city. Wisconsin is known as the **Badger State** not because of the badgers that live there, but to miners who burrowed like badgers into the hillsides in search of lead in the 1820s.

According to the 1990 census, Wisconsin had 4,891,769 inhabitants. Whites made up 92.2 percent of the population and blacks, 5 percent; additional population groups included 38,986 Native Americans, 7,354 people of Chinese origin, 5,618 people of Korean origin, 6,914 people of Indian origin, and 3,690 people of Filipino origin. Approximately 93,200 state residents are of Hispanic origin. Roman Catholics and Lutherans form the largest religious groups.

Other tidbits: The southwestern part of Wisconsin is part of the Driftless Region, in which outwash materials from melting glaciers filled most of the valleys. It is one of the most rugged and scenic areas of the state. About 43 percent of Wisconsin's land area is covered with forest, most of which is in the northern part of the state. Today, a large part of the north remains in growth forests that produce pulpwood and lumber.

The capital is Madison. The state bird is the robin; the state tree, sugar maple; and the state flower, the purple violet.

The Person(s)

Mr. Marvin Schwan

Wauwatosa. Mr. Marvin Schwan, founder of Schwan's Sales Enterprises, began in the ice cream business. When his business had grown out as far as it could on its own, he embarked on a strategy of careful acquisitions, to distribute other food products directly to his customers. He decided that pizza was not a fad, and he purchased the Tony's pizza brand and plant in Salina, Kansas. In time, he became a market share leader in frozen pizza, both for home delivery and to grocers and schools.

Mr. Schwan effectively controlled a fortune of at least $1.3 billion when he died in May 1993. He also effectively blocked his three sons and a daughter, all of whom either worked at Schwan's or have a spouse who does, from taking control of the company, while making sure that they and their heirs would be well taken care of financially. Upon his death, Mr. Schwan willed the majority of his estate—stock valued at $870 million—to a charitable religious foundation run by his former college roommate.

The foundation that received the large donation from Mr. Marvin Schwan was Wisconsin Lutheran College, founded as a two-year college in rented classrooms in 1973. It is affiliated with perhaps the most conservative of the large Lutheran sects, the Wisconsin Evangelical Lutheran Synod. It has only 321 students, 31 full-time faculty members, and a $6.8 million annual budget.

Mr. Schwan had given gifts prior to forming his foundation, including a total of $6.5 million to Bethany and a $3 million gift to Wisconsin Lutheran College in the late 1980s for a library and computer laboratory. His foundation is also known to be a supporter of Lutheran Church Missouri Synod's World Relief program which distributes humanitarian aid. The Synod is based in the St. Louis area. It supports various other missionary programs, including those of the Wisconsin Synod.

The Program(s)

TRIO

Green Bay. TRIO is a series of federally-funded programs established to help low-income Americans enter college and graduate. The programs are funded under Title IV of the Higher Education Act of 1965. Working in conjunction with student financial aid programs that help students overcome financial barriers to higher education, the TRIO programs help students overcome class, social, academic, and cultural barriers to education.

Currently, there are five federally-funded TRIO programs, of which the University of Wisconsin (Green Bay) sponsors three: Upward Bound, Student Support Services, and the Upward Bound Regional Center for Mathematics and Science. The programs share a commitment to assisting students who, by reason of socio-economic station, ethnic definition, disability, and/or restricted cultural educational experiences, find themselves in a position of disadvantaged in their pursuit of post-secondary educational opportunity. The majority of students served by the University of Wisconsin (Green Bay) TRIO programs come from households with incomes under $24,000 (family of four), where neither parent graduated from college. The University of Wisconsin (Green Bay) TRIO programs include

Regional Center for Mathematics and Science. The program currently serves 50 students from a six state region in the Upper Midwest.

Student Support Services. It currently serves 275 low-income, first-generation college students with a service array that includes skill development, coursework, tutoring, academic and career/vocational counseling.

Upward Bound. The program currently serves 55 students from Green Bay East and Green Bay West high schools .

♦ ♦ ♦

References

Schafer, L. (1995, September). Marvin Schwan's dying wish: $870 million to a religious foundation. *Corporate Report*, pp. 24-28.

Wisconsin. *World book encyclopedia.* (1998 ed.).

Website

http://www.gbms01.uwgb.edu/upbound

APPENDIX

PROGRAMS DESIGNED TO HELP PEOPLE

COLORADO

Colorado Emergency Services Volunteer Recruitment, Division of Fire Safety, 700 Kipling Street, Suite 1000, Denver, Colorado 80215; Telephone Number(s): (303 239-5704, (303) 239-4405.

Designed to recruit volunteers for the emergency service program in the state of Colorado. There is a shortage of trained volunteers who could be available in case of a serious emergency.

♦ ♦ ♦

Denver Opportunity for Outreach and Reflection (DOOR), 430 W. 9th Avenue, Denver, Colorado 80204; Telephone Number(s): (303) 937-8943, (303) 937-8942-fax.

Participants work in and learn about life in the urban environment. Emphasis is placed on understanding the circumstances of poverty and reflecting on the call to Christian service.

♦ ♦ ♦

Kempe Children's Center, 1825 Marion Street, Denver, Colorado 80218; Telephone Number(s): (303) 864-5252, (303) 864-5179-fax.

Designed to fight in the prevention of child abuse and neglect and improve the recognition and treatment of all forms of abuse.

COLORADO

Human Services Assessment Project, Department of Social Work, Colorado State University, Fort Collins, Colorado 80523; Telephone Number(s): (970) 491-5211, (970) 491-2306.

This is a research outreach program at the Department of Social Work at Colorado State University. It provides research assistance to community programs and organizations and seeks to include the expertise of social work faculty as well as the learning needs of graduate students.

♦ ♦ ♦

Denver Opportunity for Outreach and Reflection (DOOR), 430 W. 9th Avenue, Denver, Colorado 80204; Telephone Number(s): (303) 937-8943, (303) 937-8942-fax.

Participants work in and learn about life in the urban environment. Emphasis is placed on understanding the circumstances of poverty and reflecting on the call to Christian service.

♦ ♦ ♦

Colorado Information Network for Community Health (CINCH), CINCH Database Coordinator, 4300 Cherry Creek Drive South, Denver, Colorado 80222-1530; Telephone Number(s): (303) 692-2608.

Designed to provide the community with an access to a comprehensive listing and description of Colorado's health promotion programs and materials available by loan, purchase, or referral.

APPENDIX

DELAWARE

Government Relations, New Castle County, Chamber of Commerce, County Commerce Office Park, P. O. Box 11247, Wilmington, Delaware 19850; Telephone Number(s): (302) 737-4343, (302) 737-8450.

Provides an efficient and effective way for members to get involved in important issues at all levels of local government without having to devote long amounts of time that will be better spent running their businesses.

♦ ♦ ♦

Delaware Autistic Program, 144 Brennen Drive, Newark, Delaware 19713; Telephone Number(s): (302) 454-2202, (302) 454-5427-fax.

It is a public school program serving students with an educational classification of autism. Provides center-based and integrated services to over 250 students throughout the state of Delaware.

♦ ♦ ♦

Delaware Center for Teacher Education, 201 Willard Hall Education Building, University of Delaware, Newark, Delaware 19716; Telephone Number(s): (302) 831-3000, (302) 831-2708-fax.

Helps students to explore their interests in teacher education and links the research and resources of the university with the professional development needs of the Delaware education community.

IDAHO

Log Cabin Literary Center, 801 S. Capitol Boulevard, P. O. Box 9447, Boise, Idaho 83707; Telephone Number(s) (208) 331-8000.

Designed for readers and writers. This program is geared at people living in Boise. Its mission is to broaden the awareness, appreciation, and understanding of literature and to support writers and readers in their literary endeavors.

♦ ♦ ♦

Preschooler, Parents and Partners in Family Literacy, (Address Unavailable), Telephone Number(s): (208) 385-4240.

Geared at helping low-income children working below grade level. The volunteers are usually high school students.

♦ ♦ ♦

Project Love, P. O. Box 2000, Charlottetown, PEI; Canada LCA 7N8; Telephone Number(s): (902) 368-4695.

Finds older or retired volunteers to help students in school with reading and other school skills.

IOWA

Southern Prairie Area Education Agency 15, 2814 North Court Street, Olluniwa, Iowa 52501-1194; Telephone Number(s): (515) 682-8591, 1-800-622-0027, (515) 682-9083-fax.

Designed to equalize the services provided to students in an educational setting.

♦ ♦ ♦

Epilepsy Foundation of Nebraska and Iowa, 6910 Pacific Street, Suite 103, Omaha, Nebraska 68106; Telephone Number(s): (402) 553-6567.

APPENDIX 175

Helps people who are affected by epilepsy.

♦ ♦ ♦

Family Advocates, Incorporated, P. O. Box 705, Platterville, Wisconsin 53818. Telephone Number(s): (608) 348-5995.

Primarily serves residents of Grant, Iowa and Wisconsin. Provides services for victims of domestic abuse and assault.

♦ ♦ ♦

United Way of Central Iowa, 111 Ninth Street, Suite 100, Des Moines, Iowa 50314; Telephone Number(s): (515) 246-6500, (515) 246-6522-fax.

A voluntary, non-profit organization that brings together community volunteers and agencies to provide health and human services to people who live and/or work in central Iowa.

INDIANA

Welfare Policy Center, 5395 Emerson Way, Indianapolis, Indiana 46226; Telephone Number(s): (317) 549-4102.

Conducts research and provides technical assistance on welfare reform.

♦ ♦ ♦

Assistance League of Indianapolis, 1475 W. 86th Street, Suite E, Indianapolis, Indiana 46260. Telephone Number(s): (317) 872-1010.

A non-profit volunteer service organization which helps needy children and adults in the Indianapolis area.

♦ ♦ ♦

Indiana Prevention Resource Center, 2735 E. 10th Street, Room 110, Bloomington, Indiana 47408-2606; Telephone Number(s): (812) 855-1237.

Statewide clearinghouse of prevention technical assistance and information about all types of drugs.

♦ ♦ ♦

Grant County Economic Growth Council, 301 South Adams Street, Marion, Indiana 46952-3895; Telephone Number(s): (765) 662-0650.

Provides business and economic assistance to firms looking to locate in central Indiana.

KANSAS

The Northeast Kansas Education Service Center, 601 Woodson, P. O. Box 320, LeCompton, Kansas 66050; Telephone Number(s): (785)-876-7117.

An educational program that provides a network of regional educational resources to develop, implement, and maintain cooperative programs, products, and services that meet the common and unique needs of participating districts.

♦ ♦ ♦

Kosh Crime Commission, Kosh Crime Institute, 714 SW Jackson, Topeka, Kansas 66603; Telephone Number(s): (785) 375-5624, 1-800-375-5624, (785) 234-5766-fax.

A juvenile offender program in Kansas. Targets youth already in the juvenile justice system; focuses on especially troublesome population such as substance abusers, sex offenders or violent offenders. Offers services in academic/education, education/employment, individual/family/group counseling, mediation, and mentoring.

◆ ◆ ◆

Make-A-Wish Foundation of Kansas, 2016 North Amidon, Wichita, Kansas 67203; Telephone Number(s): (316)264-9474, 1-800-566-9467, (316) 832-1108-fax.

Designed to grant wishes to kids with life-threatening illnesses. Because many of these kids' lives are based around hospital stays and unpleasant discomfort, the program aims to bring some type of joy to the kids and their families.

KENTUCKY

Non-graded Education, Northwest Regional Education Laboratories, 101 SW Main, Suite 500, Portland, Oregon 97204; Telephone Number(s): (503) 275-9500.

Kentucky's legislature mandates calls for development of non-graded programs for all public school students in kindegarten through grade three. Also serves the Oregon area.

◆ ◆ ◆

WKLU TV Program, One Big Redway, Bowling Green, Kentucky 42101; Telephone Number(s): (502) 745-5371.

An educational television station.

The Outdoor Classroom Program, Crooked River Elementary School, 1820 Spur 40, St. Mary, Georgia 31558; Telephone (912) 673-6995, (912) 882-2761-fax.

Promotes investigations into the students' understanding of the ecosystem.

♦ ♦ ♦

DISC The Kentucky Museum, Western Kentucky University, Bowling Green, Kentucky 42101; Telephone Number(s): (502) 745-2592.

A program with a mission of providing educational opportunities for college, secondary, and elementary students, as well as the general public.

♦ ♦ ♦

KETV/Kentucky ETV Network, 600 Cooper Drive, Lexington, Kentucky 40502; Telephone Number(s): (606) 258-7279, (606) 258-7390.

An educational television program.

♦ ♦ ♦

First Step Home, 420 South Broadway, Lexington, Kentucky 40508; Telephone Number(s): (606) 231-6396.

For women and families in recovery.

♦ ♦ ♦

The Healing Place, 1020 West Market Street, Louisville, Kentucky 40202; Telephone Number(s): (502) 584-6606.

Designed for the homeless.

MASSACHUSETTS

Lloydminister Transition House, 8936 Commingling Street, Relind, Massachusetts 20388; Telephone Number(s): (403) 975-0966.

Helps battered women and children from abused environments.

♦ ♦ ♦

Self-Reliance Corporation, P. O. Box 3203, Waguoit, Massachusetts 02536-3203; Telephone Number(s): (888) 808-0120.

A non-profit organization devoted to helping the Massachusetts community. Citizens become self-reliant. Offers research and direct service.

♦ ♦ ♦

ARC Massachusetts, 217 South Street, Waltham, Massachusetts 02205; Telephone Number(s): (781) 891-8270.

Organization dedicated to helping individuals who are classified as mentally retarded. Promotes the general welfare of persons with mental retardation in the home, community, and institution.

MICHIGAN

Women's Health Resource Center, 1342 Taubman Center, Ann Arbor, Michigan 48109-0384; Telephone Number(s): (734) 936-8886.

Designed to improve access to coordinated comprehensive, compassionate health care for women, while contributing to social change and policy.

Muslim Community Association (MCA), 2301 Plymouth Road, Ann Arbor, Michigan 48105; Telephone Number(s): (313) 665-6772.

Helps brothers and sisters congregate for prayer. Has a full-time school and stresses Islam as a way of life.

♦ ♦ ♦

Michigan Manufacturing Technology, 2901 Hubbard Road, P. O. Box 1485, Ann Arbor, Michigan 48106-1485; Telephone Number(s): 1-800-292-4484.

Mission is to enhance the global competitiveness of Michigan's small and mid-sized manufactures. Provides training and assistance to help companies meet customer's needs.

MONTANA

Montana Workers' Compensation Board, 5 South Chance Gulch, Helena, Montana 59601; Telephone Number(s): (406) 444-6518.

Allows employees to be able to receive pay for reasons of disabilities.

♦ ♦ ♦

Montana Advocacy Program, P. O. Box 1680, Helena, Montana 59624; Telephone Number(s): (406) 444-3889.

Protects and advocates the human and legal rights of Montanans with mental and physical disabilities.

♦ ♦ ♦

Montana Department of Corrections, 1539 11th Avenue, Helena, Montana 59620; Telephone Number(s): (406) 444-5671.

APPENDIX   181

Administers the Interstate Compact on juveniles and supervises a transition center and a youth evaluation center.

NEBRASKA

Nebraska School to Career, 301 Centennial Mall South, P. O. Box 94666, Lincoln, Nebraska 68509-46666; Telephone Number(s): (402) 471-6284, 1-800-426-6505.

Education and employment opportunities enabling students to move smoothly from school to careers.

♦ ♦ ♦

Teammates of Nebraska, 301 Centennial Offices, P. O. Box 94666, Lincoln, Nebraska 68509-46666; Telephone Number(s): (402) 471-8224.

While being paired with a caring adult, children have a better chance of succeeding in school and as citizens.

♦ ♦ ♦

Entrepreneurs of the Future Camp, Lincoln Camp, 209 CBA, Lincoln, Nebraska 68588-0487; Telephone Number(s): (402) 472-0746.

Gives students a place to develop their ideas and learn about the basic fundamentals.

PENNSYLVANIA

School Age Child Care Project, Montgomery Early Learning Center, 201 Sabine Avenue, Narberth, Pennsylvania 19072; Telephone Number(s): (610) 617-4550.

Encourages the development and expansion of high quality, innovative, school-age child care programs that are affordable and accessible to working families in Philadelphia.

♦ ♦ ♦

Pennsylvania Coalition Against Rape, 1233 Locust Street, Suite 202, Philadelphia, Pennsylvania 19107; Telephone Number(s): (215) 985-3315, (215) 985-3333.

An advocate on behalf of sexual violence.

♦ ♦ ♦

The Speaking Connection, 9 Downing Drive, Dallas, Pennsylvania 18612; Telephone Number(s): (570) 675-8956, 1-800-807-0759.

Mission is to become the primary resource for continually improving communication ability. The professionals develop and deliver innovative programs designed to promote life-long learning.

RHODE ISLAND

Ocean State Free Net, Rhode Island Office of Higher Education, 301 Promenade Street, Providence, Rhode Island 02908; Telephone Number(s): (404-277-2202, (401) 277-2685.

A community computing network for Rhode Island citizens, businesses, and government.

♦ ♦ ♦

Rhode Island Guild of Home Teachers (RIGHT), P. O. Box 25, Hope, Rhode Island 02831; Telephone Number(s): Unavailable.

APPENDIX

Organization consisting of some 250 home-schooling families in Rhode Island and Southern Massachusetts, all devoted to providing their children with the highest quality of education at home.

VIRGINIA

Kids Count, People's Building, 1791 Summers Street, Suite 221, Charleston, West Virginia 25031; Telephone Number(s): (304) 543-7268.

Designed to help improve the lives of at-risk children.

♦ ♦ ♦

Youth At-Risk Community Project, West Virginia University, 815 Mallory Road, Dunbar, West Virginia 25064-2141; Telephone Number(s): (304) 768-1212, (304) 768-6912-fax.

Provides daycare, tutoring, and other programs for at-risk youths living in federal public housing.

♦ ♦ ♦

Center for Professional Development, People's Building, 1791 Summers Street, Suite 223, Charleston, West Virginia 25301; Telephone Number(s): (304) 558-0539, (304) 558-0989.

Dedicated to studying the quality of teaching and management.